Cool Restaurants
New York

teNeues

Editor:	Cynthia Reschke
Editorial coordination:	Haike Falkenberg
New York Production:	Désirée von la Valette
Layout & Pre-press:	Emma Termes Parera
Introduction text:	Cynthia Reschke
English Translation:	Robert J. Nusbaum
German Translation:	Anette Hilgendag
French Translation:	Marion Westerhoff
Spanish Translation:	Almudena Sasiain, Loft Publications

Food's photographs: © James Christopher Kendi

Photographs: Pep Escoda p. 16, 120, Björg Photography p. 56, Rockwell Group p. 124, Scott Frances p. 130, Michael Moran p. 22, Francine Fleischer Photography p. 50, Laurence Veto Galud p. 62, James Christopher Kendi p. 32, 46, 66, 84, 90, 98, 106, Matthu Placec p. 42, Yock Esto (2 photos), Suba p. 114, Gregory Goode p. 76, Jacques Caillaut p. 94, Laura Resen p. 10, Lever House p. 72, Michael Kleinberg p. 28, Paul Warchol/ Rockwell Group p. 110, Norman McGrath p. 80, Minh + Wass, Tamara Schlesinger p. 102, Rich Ventura p. 36

Published by teNeues Publishing Group
teNeues Publishing Company
16 West 22nd Street, New York, NY 10010, USA
Tel.: 001-212-627-9090, Fax: 001-212-627-9511

teNeues Book Division
Kaistraße 18
40221 Düsseldorf, Germany
Tel.: 0049-(0)211-994597-0, Fax: 0049-(0)211-994597-40

teNeues Publishing UK Ltd.
P.O. Box 402
West Byfleet
KT14 7ZF, Great Britain
Tel.: 0044-1932-403509, Fax: 0044-1932-403514

www.teneues.com

ISBN: 3-8238-4571-3

© 2003 teNeues Verlag GmbH + Co. KG, Kempen

Printed in Italy

Bibliographic information published by Die Deutsche Bibliothek.
Die Deutsche Bibliothek lists this publication in the Deutsche Nationalbibliografie; detailed bibliographic data is available in the Internet at http://dnb.ddb.de.

Content   Page

In New York, you can taste the whole world. The Big Apple offers an endless variety of restaurants serving an unimaginably wide range of dishes from different cultures. Whether it's authentic barbecued steak, lamb shanks, sushi, tapas, classic Italian cooking or the finest French cuisine, the bounty of the city's menus will sate any appetite, large or small. New York gives you everything your heart desires, from sidewalk hot dogs to gourmet meals in five-star restaurants. It's a place where the tried and true hamburger and world-class chefs compete head to head.

Newcomers to the Big Apple are overwhelmed by the range of culinary choice, whereas veteran New Yorkers focus on keeping their restaurant lists rigorously up to date. Since getting a table can be difficult, you should make a reservation weeks in advance at places like Lever House—although if you're pressed for time, you can always grab a Big Mac. Lunch at Balthazar feels like a brief sojourn in Paris, while Bungalow 8 offers a delightful tropical atmosphere complete with cocktails served under palm trees. Really hip Lenox Lounge once echoed to the strains of Billie Holiday and Miles Davis, and Malcolm X used to have a grand old time there. And you should also make a point of stopping by Coral Room for a *digestif*, and if you are lucky you'll be treated to the thrilling spectacle of mermaids cavorting in an aquarium amongst colorful fish and coral.

Delightful architecture and interior design abound, and carefully composed decors make for the loveliest of eye candy. In establishments presided over by master chefs, luminaries such as Richard Meier, Philip Wu and David Rockwell have gone to great lengths to enchant diners. Their design finesse is the icing on the cake for the creations of top chefs such as Alain Ducasse, Geoffrey Zakarian and Jean-Georges Vongerichten. In New York, haute cuisine and dining by design go hand in hand.

The pages that follow take you on a pictorial tour of 26 carefully selected restaurants in the world's most cosmopolitan city, affording you a unique behind the scenes look at how celebrated chefs work. They have shared with us the recipes for their house specialities, thus extending to you an irresistible invitation to enjoy New York's culinary atmosphere in the comfort of your own home.

In New York schmeckt man die ganze Welt! Der Big Apple bietet unendlich viele Restaurants mit den mannigfaltigsten Speisen unterschiedlicher Kulturen. Ob ein authentisches BBQ-Steak oder eine zünftige Lammhaxe, Sushi oder Tapas, klassische italienische Gerichte oder feinste französische Spezialitäten – die Fülle der Speisekarten stillt den großen und den kleinen Hunger. Man findet alles, was das Herz begehrt, vom Hot Dog auf der Straße bis hin zum Gourmet-Dinner im 5-Sterne-Restaurant – kurzum, der wohlbekannte Hamburger konkurriert mit den besten Köchen der Erde.

Neuankömmlinge sind überwältigt von der Vielfalt des Angebots, während Ansässige damit beschäftigt sind, ihre Liste stets auf dem aktuellsten Stand zu halten. Es ist oft schwierig, einen Tisch zu bekommen, darum sollte man zum Beispiel im Lever House Wochen im Voraus reservieren und wenn es schnell gehen muss, schnappt man sich eben einen Burger bei McDonald's. Kehrt man zum Mittagstisch bei Balthazar ein, ist man für kurze Zeit nach Paris versetzt, unter Palmen bei einem Cocktail im Bungalow 8 kann man tropisches Ambiente genießen, in der hippen Lenox Lounge spielten einst Billie Holiday und Miles Davis, während Malcolm X dort sein Unwesen getrieben hat. Und lieber spät als nie taucht man ab in den Coral Room zu einem Digestif. Wenn man Glück hat, erlebt man dort das aufregende Spektakel der Badenixen, die sich in einem Aquarium zwischen bunten Fischen und Korallen tummeln.

Das Auge isst mit und genießt Architektur und Interieur, die sorgfältig ausgewählte Dekoration zergeht sozusagen auf den Pupillen. Wo die Meister der Kochkunst regieren, haben Größen wie Richard Meier, Philip Wu oder David Rockwell ihr übriges getan, um die Gäste zu verzaubern. Ihr Können unterstreicht die Kreationen von Starchefs wie Alain Ducasse, Geoffrey Zakarian oder Jean-Georges Vongerichten. Haute Cuisine und dining by design gehen Hand in Hand.

Die folgenden Seiten zeigen 26 sorgfältig ausgewählte Restaurants der Weltmetropole und bieten die einmalige Gelegenheit, hinter die Kulissen gefeierter Köche zu blicken. Sie verraten uns die Rezepte der Spezialität des Hauses und verführen dazu, im eigenen Heim die kulinarische Atmosphäre New Yorks nachzuempfinden.

A New York, on goûte aux saveurs du monde entier ! La Big Apple offre un nombre infini de restaurants avec les plats les plus variés issus de cultures différentes. Que ce soit un vrai steak pour barbecue ou un jarret de mouton bien consistant, des sushis ou des tapas, des plats classiques de la cuisine italienne ou des spécialités les plus fines de la cuisine française – l'abondance des menus permet d'apaiser toutes les faims, les petites comme les grandes. Chacun y trouve son bonheur, du hot-dog pris dans la rue au dîner de gourmet dans un restaurant 5 étoiles – bref, le fameux hamburger rivalise avec les meilleurs cuisiniers de la terre.

Si les nouveaux venus sont subjugués par la variété de l'offre, les résidents sont occupés par la constante mise à jour de leur liste. Comme il est souvent difficile de trouver une table, chez Lever House, par exemple, il est préférable de réserver des semaines à l'avance. Mais pour faire vite, on avale un hamburger chez McDonald's. Chez Balthazar, on est transporté à Paris, le temps d'un déjeuner. Au Bungalow 8, on savoure un cocktail sous les palmiers dans une ambiance tropicale, et c'est au Lenox Lounge, club branché, que jouait autrefois Billie Holiday et Miles Davis et où Malcolm X faisait des siennes. Et enfin, mieux vaut tard que jamais pour plonger dans le Coral Room afin d'y prendre un digestif. Avec un peu de chance, on assiste au spectacle excitant de naïades qui s'ébattent dans un aquarium au milieu de coraux et de poissons multicolores.

C'est un régal pour les yeux qui se délectent d'architecture et d'intérieurs. La décoration soigneusement choisie fait pour ainsi dire fondre de plaisir. Là où les maîtres de l'art culinaire sont rois, les grands noms tels que Richard Meier, Philip Wu ou David Rockwell se sont dépassés pour enchanter la clientèle. Leur savoir-faire rehausse les créations des stars de la cuisine comme Alain Ducasse, Geoffrey Zakarian ou Jean-Georges Vongerichten. Haute cuisine et dîner dans un cadre design vont de pair.

Les pages suivantes montrent 26 restaurants de la métropole mondiale, soigneusement sélectionnés, et donnent l'occasion unique de jeter un coup d'œil derrière les coulisses de cuisiniers célèbres. En nous dévoilant les recettes de la spécialité de la maison, ils nous incitent à retrouver chez nous, l'ambiance culinaire de New York.

En Nueva York se puede saborear todo el mundo! La Gran Manzana ofrece infinidad de restaurantes con variadísimas recetas de todas las culturas. Desde un auténtico filete a la parrilla o una contundente pata de cordero, hasta sushi, tapas, recetas italianas clásicas o las más finas especialidades francesas: la abundancia de menús es suficiente para satisface grandes apetitos y pequeños antojos. En Nueva York se encuentra todo lo que se desee, desde un perrito caliente en un puesto callejero hasta cenas de gourmet en restaurantes de 5 estrellas; en una palabra, en esta ciudad la archiconocida hamburguesa compite con los mejores cocineros del mundo.

Los recién llegados se sienten algo intimidados por la variedad de la oferta, mientras que los autóctonos tienen bastante con estar al día de las novedades. A veces es muy difícil conseguir una mesa, por ejemplo en Lever House hay que hacer la reserva con semanas de anticipación, pero cuando es necesario darse prisa, la gente se va a comer una hamburguesa al McDonald's. Quien acude al mediodía a Balthazar, se siente transplantado durante rato en París, mientras que si se entra en Bungalow 8 se puede disfrutar de un cóctel bajo las hojas de las palmeras y en un ambiente tropical. En el actualísimo Lenox Lounge tocaron una vez Billie Holiday y Miles Davis, y allí también hizo de las suyas Malcolm X. Y mejor tarde que nunca, se puede uno dejar caer en Coral Room para tomar un aperitivo. Si se tiene suerte, se podrá disfrutar del espectáculo de las ninfas marinas, que bucean entre peces y corales.

La mirada se recrea con la arquitectura y el interiorismo; la cuidada decoración es un placer que se saborea con los ojos. Allí donde reinan los maestros del arte culinario, genios como Richard Meier, Philip Wu o David Rockwell se ponen también al servicio de los comensales. Su talento subraya las creaciones de grandes chefs como Alain Ducasse, Geoffrey Zakarian o Jean-Georges Vongerichten. En estos locales, la alta cocina y el mejor diseño se dan la mano. Las siguientes páginas muestran 26 restaurantes escogidos de la metrópoli internacional y ofrecen la oportunidad única de contemplar a los cocineros entre bastidores. Ellos nos confían sus recetas de la especialidad de la casa y nos inducen a recrear en nuestro hogar la atmósfera culinaria de Nueva York.

Balthazar

Owner: Keith McNally | Chef: Riad Nasr and Lee Hanson

80 Spring Street | New York, NY 10012
Phone: +1 212 965 1414
www.balthazarny.com
Subway: N, R, W to Prince Street, 6 to Spring Street
Opening hours: Mon–Fri 7:30 am to 11:30 am, noon to 5 pm, 5:45 pm to
1:30 am, Fri until 2:30 am, Sat 7:30 am to 3:30 pm, 5:45 pm to 2:30 am,
Sun 7:30 am to 3:30 pm, 5:30 pm to midnight
Average price: Breakfast $3 – $6, Lunch $9 – $22, Dinner $16 – $24
Cuisine: Traditional French Brasserie

Frisée

aux Lardons

Friséesalat mit Speck
Frisée aux Lardons
Escarola con panceta

L ✓

6 slices of stale brioche • 4 heads of fri-sée, cored, rinsed, spun dry, and torn into bite-size pieces • 1 tsp plus 1/2 cup sherry vinegar • 1/2 lb slab bacon, cut into 1/2-inch lardoons • 4 shallots, peeled and minced (about 1/2 cup) • 1/2 cup olive oil • 1/2 tsp salt, plus more to taste • 1/4 tsp freshly ground black pepper, plus more to taste • 3 tbsp fines herbes • 6 large eggs • sea salt

Trim the crusts from the bread and cut into 1/2-inch cubes. Place into a sheet tray and bake in the oven until golden brown, about 10 minutes. Combine the croutons in a large bowl with the clean frisée.

In a dry skillet or sauté pan over medium heat, brown the lardoons well on all sides about 10 minutes. Add the minced shallots and continue to cook for 2 to 3 minutes, to soften and lightly brown them. Without pouring off the fat, add the 1/2 cup of vinegar to the pan. Bring to a boil, using a wooden spoon to scrape any delicious bits that have caramelised on the surface of the pan. When the vinegar has reduced by half, about 3 minutes, turn off the flame. Add the olive oil, salt and pepper, and stir well to combine. Pour this warm vinaigrette with bacon into the bowl of frisée, along with the croutons and fines herbes. Toss well to combine.

Crack the eggs, one at a time, into a small saucer and then slide them into simmering water. Poach for 4 minutes, resulting in a set white and a cooked but runny yolk. With a slotted spoon, scoop out the poached eggs, one at a time, drain, and position on top of each pile of frisée. Sprinkle with crunchy sea salt and a few turns of a peppermill. Serve immediately.

6 Scheiben alte Briochebrötchen • 4 Köpfe Frisée-Salat, Inneres entfernen, waschen, trocken schleudern und in kleine Stücke reißen • 1 TL und 1/2 Tasse Sherryessig • 250 g Schinkenspeck in Würfel geschnitten • 4 Schalotten, geschält und gehackt (ca. 1/2 Tasse) • 1/2 Tasse Olivenöl • 1/2 TL Salz, nach Geschmack • 1/4 TL frisch gemahlener schwarzer Pfeffer, nach Geschmack • 3 EL Kräutermischung • 6 große Eier • Meersalz

Rinde von den Brötchen abschneiden und in Würfel schneiden. Auf ein Backblech legen und ca. 10 Minuten goldbraun backen. Die Croutons in einer großen Schüssel mit gewaschenem und getrocknetem Frisée-Salat mischen.

In einer trockenen Pfanne oder Kasserolle den Speck auf mittlerer Hitze von allen Seiten für etwa 10 Minuten anbraten. Die gehackten Schalotten dazugeben und 2 bis 3 Minuten anbraten, bis sie weich und leicht angebräunt sind. Ohne das Fett abzugießen, 1/2 Tasse Essig in die Pfanne geben. Aufkochen lassen und mit einem Holzlöffel Angebackenes vom Pfannenboden kratzen. Den Essig in ca. 3 Minuten auf die Hälfte reduzieren und Kochplatte ausstellen. Olivenöl, Salz und Pfeffer dazugeben, gut umrühren. Die warme Vinaigrette mit Speck in die Salatschüssel über den Frisée und die Croutons geben und die Kräutermischung darüber streuen. Gut vermischen.

Eier nacheinander in einen kleinen Topf geben und in siedendes Wasser gleiten lassen. 4 Minuten pochieren, bis das Weiße fest, das Eigelb aber noch flüssig ist. Mit einem Schaumlöffel die pochierten Eier nacheinander herausnehmen und auf die Friséehäufchen legen. Mit Meersalz und frischem Pfeffer würzen. Sofort servieren.

6 tranches de brioche rassie • 4 frisées,
lavées, rincées, essorées et coupées en
petits morceaux • 1 c. à café plus 1/2
tasse de vinaigre de sherry • 250 g de lard
fumé coupé en lardons • 4 échalotes
pelées et émincées (environ 1/2 tasse) •
1/2 tasse d'huile d'olive • 1/2 c. à café de
sel et plus pour rectifier • 1/4 c. à café de
poivre noir frais moulu et plus pour rectifier •
3 c. à soupe de fines herbes • 6 gros œufs •
sel de mer

Enlevez la croûte du pain et coupez en dés.
Mettez sur une plaque et dorez au four 10
minutes environ. Dans un grand bol, mélangez les croûtons à la frisée lavée.

Faites bien revenir les lardons pendant
environ 10 minutes dans une poêle. Ajoutez
l'échalote émincée et continuez à cuire pendant 2 à 3 minutes, pour les dorer légèrement. Sans ôter le gras, ajoutez 1/2 tasse
de vinaigre. Amenez à ébullition et grattez
avec une cuillère en bois tous les délicieux
petits bouts caramélisés. Une fois que le
vinaigre a réduit de 1/2, au bout de 3
minutes environ, éteindre le feu. Ajoutez
l'huile d'olive, le sel et le poivre et mélangez vivement. Versez cette vinaigrette chaude avec les lardons dans le bol de frisée
avec les croûtons et les fines herbes.
Mélangez bien.

Cassez les œufs, l'un après l'autre dans
une petite saucière et laissez-les glisser
dans l'eau frémissante. Faites pocher pendant 4 minutes afin d'obtenir un blanc dur
et un jaune cuit mais mou. Avec une écumoire, retirez les œufs l'un après l'autre,
égouttez et déposez-les sur chaque tas de
frisée. Saupoudrez de sel de mer et de
quelques tours de moulin à poivre. Servez
immédiatement.

6 panecillos duros • 4 escarolas limpias,
escurridas y cortadas • 1 cucharadita y
1/2 taza de vinagre • 250 g de panceta
cortada en daditos • 4 cebolletas peladas •
1/2 taza de aceite de oliva • sal • pimienta negra • 3 cucharadas de finas hierbas •
6 huevos grandes • sal marina

Trocear los panecillos en pedazos muy
pequeños y tostar al horno hasta que estén
dorados. Una vez listos, depositarlos en un
recipiente con la escarola.

En una sartén, saltear la panceta unos 10
minutos. Añadir las cebolletas y continuar
la cocción durante 2 o 3 minutos hasta que
estén blanditos y ligeramente dorados.
Agregar el vinagre y llevar a ebullición utili-
zando una cuchara de madera para despe-
gar los dados de panceta que se vayan
caramelizando. Cuando el vinagre se ha
reducido a la mitad (después de unos 3
minutos), apagar el fuego, añadir el aceite
de oliva, la sal, la pimienta y remover bien.
Verter este preparado en el recipiente
donde se había reservado la escarola, y aliñar con finas hierbas. Mezclar bien.

Cascar los huevos, uno por uno, en un recipiente pequeño y pasar cuidadosamente a
una olla de agua hirviendo. Dejar cocer
durante unos 4 minutos. Sacar los huevos y
dejarlos escurrir. Depositarlos sobre la
ensalada y salpimentar. Servir inmediatamente.

Blue Fin

Architect: Yabu Pushelberg | Chef: Paul Sale (Pastry:
Robert Valencia)

W Times Square Hotel | 1567 Broadway 47th Street | New York, NY 10036
Phone: +1 212 918 1400
www.brguestrestaurants.com
Subway: N, R, W, to 49th Street or 1 and 9 to 50th Street
Opening hours: Sun–Mon 7 am to 11 am, 11:30 am to 4 pm, 5 pm to midnight;
Tue, Thu until 12:30 am; Fri–Sat until 1 am
Average price: Appetizers: $8 – $16, Entrees: $21 – $32, Desserts: $8 – $9
Cuisine: Modern Seafood

Sesame crusted Big Eye Tuna

with Ginger Soy Vinaigrette

In Sesam gehüllter Big-Eye-Tunfisch mit Ingwer-Soja-Vinaigrette
Thon à gros œil en croûte de sésame avec vinaigrette au gingembre et soja
Atún rebozado en sésamo con vinagreta de soja con jengibre

4 x 7 oz filets big eye tuna (cut into logs) • 3 oz black and white sesame seed • 7 oz snow peas • 6 oz baby carrots • 6 oz shiitake mushrooms • 8 oz fingerling potatoes • 1 oz olive oil • 4 fl oz soy ginger vinaigrette • 8 sprigs chervil

Clean and blanch all the vegetables leaving the skin on the fingerling potatoes. Season and roll the tuna in the sesame seeds (egg and flour is NOT needed, sesame seeds will naturally stick to the fish). First sauté off the fingerling potatoes until golden brown, then add the shiitakes, carrots, and snow peas. Pour the olive oil in a hot sauté pan, then sear the tuna on all four sides and cook to desired temperature (rare or med-rare is recommended).
Place the sautéed vegetables in the center of the plate. Cut the tuna into four equal slices and place two pieces on top of the vegetable and two to the side making a straight line of tuna. Pour 1 oz. of the vinaigrette around. Garnish with the picked chervil.

Ginger soy vinaigrette (1 quart)
2 cups lite soy sauce, 1/4 cup oyster sauce, 1/4 cup champagne vinaigrette, 1 cup blended olive oil, 1/2 cup finely chopped shallots, 1/4 cup finely chopped ginger

Place all ingredients into a bowl (except olive oil) and mix together. Slowly whisk in the oil.

4 x 200 g Big-Eye-Tunfisch-Filets (in Würfel geschnitten) • 80 g schwarze und weiße Sesamkörner • 200 g Zuckererbsen • 180 g Babykarotten • 180 g Shiitake-Pilze • 250 g Fingerling-Kartoffeln • 25 g Olivenöl • 25 cl Soja-Ingwer-Vinaigrette • 8 Zweige Kerbel

Das Gemüse waschen und blanchieren, die Kartoffeln nicht schälen. Den Tunfisch salzen und pfeffern und in den Sesamkörnern rollen (Ei und Mehl ist NICHT nötig, da der Sesam direkt am Fisch haften bleibt).
Zuerst die Fingerling-Kartoffeln gold-braun anbraten, dann die Shiitake-Pilze, Karotten und Zuckererbsen hinzufügen. Das Olivenöl in eine heiße Pfanne laufen lassen und den Tunfisch von allen vier Seiten rasch anbraten (blutig oder halb-gar wird empfohlen). Die gegarten Gemüse in der Mitte des Tellers anrichten. Den Tunfisch in 4 gleich große Scheiben schneiden und 2 auf dem Gemüse und 2 daneben anrichten. 25 cl der Vinaigrette darum gießen und mit dem abgezupften Kerbel garnieren.

Ingwer-Soja-Vinaigrette (1 l)
2 Tassen helle Sojasoße, 1/4 Tasse Austernsoße, 1/4 Tasse Champagner-Vinaigrette, 1 Tasse Olivenöl, 1/2 Tasse fein gehackte Schalotten, 1/4 Tasse fein gehackter Ingwer

Alle Zutaten (außer das Olivenöl) in eine Schüssel geben und verrühren. Das Öl langsam unterschlagen.

4 x 200 g de filets de thon (coupé en morceaux) • 80 g de graines de sésame blanches et noires • 200 g de pois • 180 g de mini carottes • 180 g de champignons shiitake • 250 g de pommes de terre fingerling • 25 g d'huile d'olive • 25 cl de vinaigrette au gingembre et soja • 8 brins de cerfeuil

Nettoyez et blanchissez tous les légumes en laissant la peau des pommes de terre fingerling. Assaisonnez et roulez le thon dans les graines de sésame (PAS besoin d'utiliser ni œuf ni farine: les graines de sésame adhérent naturellement au poisson).
Faites d'abord sauter les pommes de terre fingerling jusqu'à ce qu'elles soient bien dorées et ajoutez ensuite les shiitakes, les carottes et enfin les gousses de pois chinois. Versez de l'huile d'olive dans une poêle à frire chaude, faites revenir ensuite le thon sur les quatre côtés et cuisez le à la température souhaitée (nous recommandons saignant ou mi-saignant).
Placez les légumes sautés au centre de l'assiette. Coupez le thon en quatre tranches égales. Placez ensuite deux morceaux sur les légumes et deux sur les côtés pour aligner le thon. Versez 25 cl de vinaigrette tout autour. Garnissez de brins de cerfeuil.

Vinaigrette soja-gingembre (1 l), 2 tasses de sauce soja, 1/4 de tasse de sauce d'huître, 1/4 de tasse de vinaigrette au Champagne, 1 tasse d'huile d'olive vierge, 1/2 tasse d'échalotes finement émincées, 1/4 de tasse de gingembre finement émincé

Placez tous les ingrédients dans un bol (sauf l'huile d'olive) et mélangez le tout. Ajoutez l'huile en la fouettant doucement.

4 rodajas de 200 g cada una de atún • 80 g de semillas de sésamo blancas y negras • 200 g de guisantes • 180 g de zanahorias pequeñas • 180 g de setas shiitake • 250 g de patatas nuevas • aceite de oliva • 25 cl vinagreta de soja con jengibre • 8 ramilletes de perifollo

Lavar y blanquear todas las verduras, sin mondar las patatas. Freír las patatas hasta que estén doradas y añadir las shiitakes, las zanahorias y los guisantes. Sazonar y rebozar el atún en las semillas de sésamo (NO es necesario utilizar huevo y harina, ya que las semillas de sésamo se adhieren al pescado). Vertir el aceite en una sartén bien caliente y freír el atún por los cuatro lados.
Colocar los vegetales salteados en el centro del plato. Cortar el atún en cuatro trozos iguales y colocar dos sobre las verduras y dos al lado. Aliñar con la vinagreta y adornar con los ramilletes de perifollo.

Vinagreta de soja con jengibre (1 l)
2 tazas de salsa de soja clara, 1/4 taza de salsa de ostras, 1/4 taza de vinagre de champán, 1 taza de aceite de oliva batido, 1/2 taza de cebolletas finamente picadas, 1/4 taza de jengibre finamente picado

Colocar todos los ingredientes en un cuenco, a excepción del aceite, y mezclar. Vertir el aceite lentamente.

Brasserie

Architect: Diller & Scofidio | Chef: Luc Dimnet

The Seagram Building, 100 East 53rd Street | New York, NY 10022
Phone: +1 212 751 4840
www.restaurantassociates.com/brasserie
Subway: E, F, 6 to Lexington Avenue – 51st Street
Opening hours: Breakfast Mon–Fri 7 am to 10 am, Continental Breakfast from
10 am to noon, Brunch Sat–Sun 11 am to 3:30 pm, Lunch Mon–Fri 11 am to 3 pm,
Dinner Mon–Thu 5 pm to midnight, Fri–Sat 5 pm to 1 am, Sun 5 pm to 10 pm
Average price: $15 – $32
Cuisine: French

Lamb Shank

with Polenta and dried Tomatoes

Lammhaxen mit Polenta und getrockneten Tomaten
Jarret d'agneau accompagné de polenta et de tomates séchées
Pata de cordero asada con polenta y tomates secos

For the lamb shank
4 pieces lamb shank (bone in 22 oz each) •
2 cups virgin olive oil • 1 spanish onion
diced • 1 large carrot diced • 1 head of
garlic halved • 1 bunch cilantro root • 2
piece fresh bay leaf • 2 sprigs fresh thyme •
4 tbsp tomato paste • 2 tbsp harrissa • 1
tbsp cumin powder • 2 oz red wine vinegar •
salt and pepper • 750 ml Chardonnay • 1
gallon chicken stock

Sear the lamb shanks in a large roasting
pan with virgin olive oil. Remove the lamb
shanks. In same roasting pan add all the
vegetables, spices and herbs and
caramelize. Deglaze with white wine.
Replace the lamb shanks. Completely cover
the lamb shanks and garnish with chicken
stock. Let cook in a 284 °F oven for 1 hour
and 45 minutes. Remove the lamb shanks.
Strain the stock, disgard garnish of vegetables. Reduce strained stock by 1/3. Pour
over lamb after plating.

For the mascarpone polenta and oven dried
tomatoes
1/2 cup polenta • 1 cup milk • 1/2 lb butter • 1 tsp salt • 1 pinch nutmeg • 2 tbsp
mascarpone • 4 plum tomatoes • 1 tbsp
virgin olive oil • 1 sprig Thai basil

Bring milk to boil, add butter, salt and nutmeg. Add polenta. Cook for 10 minutes
(keep stirring until completely cooked). Mix
with mascarpone.

For the oven dried tomatoes
Soak plum tomatoes in hot water for 1
minute. Peel tomatoes. Marinade tomatoes
in olive oil, chopped Thai basil, salt and
pepper. Dry tomatoes in 250 °F oven for 45
minutes.

Für die Lammhaxen
4 Lammhaxen (mit Knochen, je 660 g) •
2 Tassen natives Olivenöl • 1 spanische
Zwiebel, in Würfel geschnitten • 1 große
Karotte, in Würfel geschnitten • 1 Knob-
lauchknolle, halbiert • 1 Bündel Koriander •
2 frische Lorbeerblätter • 2 Zweige frischer
Thymian • 4 EL Tomatenmark • 2 EL
Harrissa-Gewürzpaste • 1 EL Kreuzkümmel-
pulver • 60 ml Rotweinessig • Salz und
Pfeffer • 750 ml Chardonnay • 4 l
Hühnerbrühe

Die Lammstücke in einer großen Kasserolle
in Olivenöl anbraten. Lammstücke aus der
Kasserolle nehmen. Gemüse und Kräuter in
dieselbe Kasserolle geben und karamellisie-
ren. Mit Weißwein löschen. Lammstücke wieder in die Kasserolle geben. Lammstücke,
Gemüse und Kräuter komplett mit der Hühnerbrühe bedecken. Im Ofen bei 140 °C eine
Stunde und 45 Minuten garen lassen. Lammstücke aus der Kasserolle nehmen. Brühe
passieren, Gemüse entfernen. Passierte
Brühe auf 1/3 reduzieren. Lamm auf Servier-
teller anrichten und mit Brühe übergießen.

Für die Mascarpone-Polenta und die ofengetrockneten Tomaten
1/2 Tasse Polenta • 1 Tasse Milch • 225 g
Butter • 1 TL Salz • 1 Prise Muskat • 2 EL
Mascarpone • 4 Pflaumentomaten • 1 EL
natives Olivenöl • 1 Zweig Thai-Basilikum

Milch aufkochen und Butter, Salz und
Muskat hinzugeben. Polenta dazugeben. 10
Minuten kochen (umrühren, bis Polenta voll-
kommen eingekocht ist). Mit Mascarpone
mischen.

Für die ofengetrockneten Tomaten
Pflaumentomaten 1 Minute in heißes
Wasser tauchen. Tomaten schälen. Tomaten
in Olivenöl, gehacktem Thai-Basilikum, Salz
und Pfeffer marinieren. Tomaten für 45
Minuten bei 120 °C im Ofen trocknen
lassen.

Pour le jarret d'agneau
4 morceaux de jarret d'agneau (de 660 g
chacun avec l'os) • 2 tasses d'huile d'olive
vierge • 1 gros oignon d'Espagne coupé en
dés • 1 grande carotte coupée en dés • 1
moitié de tête d'ail • 1 bouquet de racines
de cilantro • 2 feuilles de laurier frais • 2
brins de thym frais • 4 c. à soupe de concentré de tomate • 2 c. à soupe de harissa •
1 c. à soupe cumin en poudre • 60 ml de
vinaigre de vin • sel & poivre • 750 ml de
Chardonnay • 4 l de bouillon de poule

Faites revenir les jarrets d'agneau dans une
grande rôtissoire avec de l'huile d'olive vierge. Retirez les jarrets d'agneau. Ajoutez dans
la même rôtissoire tous les légumes, épices
et herbes, faites caraméliser. Déglacez avec
le vin blanc. Remettez les jarrets d'agneau.
Couvrez complètement les jarrets d'agneau,
les légumes et épices et ajoutez le bouillon
de poule. Faites cuire au four à 140 °C pendant 1 heure 40 minutes. Retirez les jarrets
d'agneau. Passez le bouillon, réservez les
légumes pour garnir. Réduisez d'1/3 le
bouillon filtré. Versez sur l'agneau après l'a-
voir disposé sur un plat.

Pour la polenta au mascarpone et les tomates séchées au four
1/2 tasse de polenta • 1 tasse de lait • 225 g
de beurre • 1 c. à café de sel • 1 pincée de
noix de muscade • 2 c. à soupe de mascarpone • 4 tomates olivettes • 1 c. à soupe
d'huile d'olive vierge • 1 brin de basilic thai

Faites bouillir le lait, ajoutez le sel et la
noix de muscade. Ajoutez la polenta. Faites
cuire 10 minutes (continuer à tourner
jusqu'à cuisson complète). Mélangez avec
le mascarpone.

Pour les tomates séchées au four
Laissez tremper les tomates olivettes dans
de l'eau chaude pendant 1 minute. Pelez les
tomates. Faites mariner les tomates dans
l'huile d'olive, le basilic thai haché. Salez et
poivrez. Sécher aux four à 120 °C pendant
45 minutes.

Para el cordero
4 raciones de pata de cordero (660 g cada
uno) • 2 tazas de aceite de oliva virgen •
una cebolla picada • 1 zanahoria grande
picada • una cabeza de ajo cortada por la
mitad • una pizca de cilantro • 2 trozos de
hoja de baya fresca • dos ramilletes de
tomillo fresco • 4 cucharadas de pasta
de tomate • 2 cucharadas de harrisa • 1
cucharada de comino • 60 ml de vinagre de
vino tinto • sal y pimienta • 750 ml de vino
chardonnay • 4 l de caldo de pollo

Dorar el cordero en una sartén grande con
aceite de oliva virgen. Apartar el cordero.
En la misma sartén añadir todos las verduras, especias y hierbas, y caramelizar.
Desglasar con vino blanco. Añadir el cordero. Cubrirlo todo con caldo de pollo. Cocinar
durante 1 hora y 45 minutos en el horno a
140 °C. Reservar el cordero y colar las verduras; reducir el caldo resultante hasta
obtener un tercio del volumen. Vertir sobre
el cordero cuando esté servido.

Para la polenta de mascarpone con tomates secos
1/2 taza de polenta • 1 taza de leche •
225 g de mantequilla • 1 cucharada de sal •
1 pizca de nuez moscada • 2 cucharadas
de mascarpone (queso en crema italiano) •
4 tomates • 1 cucharada de aceite de oliva
virgen • 1 ramillete de albahaca

Llevar la leche a ebullición, añadir la mantequilla, la sal, la nuez moscada y la polenta.
Cocer durante 10 minutos, removiendo constantemente. Mezclar con el queso en crema.

Para los tomates secos
Escaldar los tomates durante un minuto,
pelarlos, salpimentarlos y adobarlos en
aceite con albahaca. Secar al horno durante 45 minutos a 120 °C.

Bungalow 8

Architect: Rafael and Diana Vinoly | Chef: Tom Dimarzo

515 West 27th Street | New York, NY 10001
Phone: +1 212 629 3333
Subway: C, E to 23rd Street
Opening hours: Mon–Sat 10 pm to 4 am
Average price: $8 – $70
Cuisine: Club (lobster club sandwich scrambled eggs with oyster caviar)

Cipriani Downtown

Chef: Team of chefs rotating for each location, travelling between Venice, NY, London, Punta del Este, Porto Cervo and Hong Kong to guarantee the same standard of quality in each Cipriani venue

376 West Broadway | New York, NY 10012
Phone: +1 212 343 0999
www.cipriani.com
Subway: C, E to Spring Street
Opening hours: Mon–Sun noon to midnight
Average price: $18–$30
Cuisine: Italian

L/D
FRANCOIS

Scampi

Alla Carlina

Shrimps à la Carlina
Shrimps à la Carlina
Gambas a la Carlina

2 1/2 lb large shrimps, peeled and deveined • salt • freshly ground pepper • flour for dredging • 4 to 6 tbsp olive oil • 1/4 cup unsalted butter, cut into bits • 1/4 cup chopped flat-leaf parsley • 1 tbsp chopped drained capers • 2 tbsp chopped unsweetened gherkins or cornichons • Worcestershire sauce • 1/4 cup tomato sauce • juice of 1/2 lemon

Wash the shrimps and dry them well with paper towels. Season with salt and pepper, dredge them in flour, and shake them in a sieve to remove excess flour. Heat the olive oil in a large skillet over medium high heat. Add the shrimps and cook them in batches, tossing constantly, for 4 to 5 minutes, until they are slightly browned and crisp. Remove the shrimps from the pan with a slotted spoon and arrange them in one layer in a shallow ovenproof dish. Pour off the oil from the skillet, add the butter and parsley, and cook for 30 seconds or so, until the butter just starts to brown. Remove the pan from the heat. Sprinkle the capers and gherkins over the shrimps, sprinkle on a few drops of Worcestershire sauce, and dot with tomato sauce. Squeeze on some lemon juice and pour the butter and parsley over all. Serve together with "White Rice Pilaf".

1,125 kg große Shrimps, geschält und ausgenommen • Salz • frisch gemahlener Pfeffer • Mehl zum Bestäuben • 4 bis 6 EL Olivenöl • 1/4 Tasse ungesalzene Butter, in Stückchen geschnitten • 1/4 Tasse glatte Petersilie, gehackt • 1 EL abgegossene Kapern, gehackt • 2 EL gehackte ungesüßte Gewürzgurken oder Cornichons • Worcestersauce • 1/4 Tasse Tomatensauce • Saft einer 1/2 Zitrone

Shrimps waschen und gut mit Küchentüchern trocknen. Mit Salz und Pfeffer würzen, in Mehl wälzen und mit Hilfe eines Siebs überschüssiges Mehl abschütteln. Olivenöl in einer großen Pfanne bei mittlerer Hitze erhitzen. Shrimps in kleinen Portionen in die Pfanne geben und jeweils 4 bis 5 Minuten braten, dabei immer wieder umrühren, bis sie leicht angebräunt und knusprig sind. Shrimps mit Schaumlöffel aus der Pfanne nehmen und in einer Schicht auf tiefen, feuerfesten Tellern verteilen. Öl aus der Pfanne gießen, die Butter und Petersilie dazugeben und etwa 30 Sekunden kochen, bis die Butter gerade anfängt braun zu werden. Pfanne vom Feuer nehmen. Die Kapern und die Gürkchen über die Shrimps streuen und ein paar Tropfen Worcestersauce und die Tomatensauce darüber verteilen. Zitronensaft auspressen und mit Butter und Petersilie über das Ganze gießen. Mit weißem „Pilawreis" servieren.

1,125 kg de grosses gambas, pelées et nettoyées • sel • poivre fraîch. moulu • farine pour saupoudrer • 4 à 6 c. à soupe d'huile d'olive • 1/4 de tasse de beurre doux coupé en dés • 1/4 de tasse de persil plat haché • 1c. à soupe de câpres hachées • 2 c. à soupe de cornichons aigres • sauce Worcestershire • 1/4 de tasse de sauce tomate • jus d'1/2 citron

Lavez les gambas et séchez-les bien avec du papier absorbant. Salez et poivrez, roulez-les dans la farine et secouez dans une passoire pour retirer l'excédent de farine. Chauffez l'huile d'olive dans une grande friteuse à feu moyen. Ajoutez les gambas et cuisez-les par paquets, en secouant constamment pendant 4 à 5 minutes, afin qu'elles soient dorées et croustillantes. Retirez les gambas de la friteuse à l'aide d'une écumoire et en mettre une couche dans un plat allant au four. Jetez l'huile de la friteuse, ajoutez le beurre et le persil et cuire pendant 30 secondes environ pour que le beurre brunisse légèrement. Retirez du feu. Eparpillez câpres et cornichons sur les gambas et ajoutez quelques gouttes de sauce Worcestershire et arrosez de sauce tomate. Arrosez de jus de citron puis versez le beurre et le persil sur le tout. Servez avec du « riz blanc pilaf ».

1,125 kg de gambas grandes, peladas y limpias • sal • pimienta fresca molida • harina para rebozar • de 4 a 6 cucharadas de aceite de oliva • 1/4 taza de mantequilla cortada en daditos • 1/4 taza de perejil picado • 1 cucharada de alcaparras escurridas y picadas • 2 cucharadas de pepinillos • salsa de Worcestershire • 1/4 taza de salsa de tomate • zumo de medio limón

Lavar y secar las gambas. Salpimentar. Rebozarlas y sacudirlas para desprender el exceso de harina. Calentar el aceite en una sartén grande a fuego medio. Agregar las gambas y cocinarlas removiéndolas constantemente durante 4 o 5 minutos, hasta que estén ligeramente tostadas y crujientes. Retirar y colocar en una fuente de horno poco profunda. Retirar el aceite de la sartén y añadir la mantequilla y el perejil; freír durante 30 segundos aproximadamente, hasta que la mantequilla comience a tostarse. Quitar la sartén del fuego. Colocar las alcaparras y los pepinillos sobre las gambas, echar unas gotas de salsa de Worcerstershire y cubrir con la salsa de tomate. Verter sobre el preparado el zumo de limón, la mantequilla y el perejil. Servir acompañado de arroz pilaf.

Coral Room

Architect: Chris Ventura and Paul Devitt

512 West 29th Street I New York, NY 10001
Phone: +1 212 244 1965
www.coralroomnyc.com, info@coralroomnyc.com
Subway: A, C, E to 34th Street/Penn Station, 1 and 9 to 28th Street
Opening hours: Mon–Sun 10 pm to 4 am
Average price: $5 – $40
Ambience: Club with live mermaid performance in 9.000 gallon aquarium

Fishbowl

Fishbowl
Bocal de poisson
Pecera

2 oz Bacardi Orange • 1 oz Apricot Brandy •
1/2 oz Blue Curaçao • 4 oz Grapefruit juice •
dash of fresh lime juice • dash of
Grenadine

Served on ice.

60 ml Bacardi Orange • 30 ml Apricot Brandy •
15 ml Blue Curaçao • 120 ml Grapefruitsaft •
1 Spritzer frischer Limettensaft • 1 Spritzer
Grenadine

Serviert auf Eis.

60 ml Bacardi Orange • 30 ml de liqueur
d'abricot • 15 ml Curaçao blue • 120 ml de
jus de pamplemousse • quelques gouttes
de jus de citron vert frais • quelques
gouttes de grenadine

Servir sur glaçons.

60 ml Bacardi Orange • 30 ml de licor de
albaricoque • 15 ml de Blue Curaçao •
120 ml de zumo de pomelo • 1 chorrito de
zumo de lima • 1 chorrito de granadina

Servir con hielo.

Glass

Architect: Leeser Architecture | Owner: Fernando Henao

287 10th Avenue | New York, NY 10001
Phone: +1 212 904 1580
www.glassloungenyc.com
Subway: 1 and 9 to 28th Street
Opening hours: Tue–Fri 6 pm to 4 am, Sat 8 pm to 4 am
Average price: $9 – $10 cocktails
Ambience: Sleek, aerodynamic lounge with a bamboo smoking garden

Cocktails

Mojito Rosa
(most popular drink—red with green
crushed mint)

1 tsp fresh raspberry puree
6–7 springs of crushed mint
1 tsp raw sugar
Cut a whole lime into slices
2 oz Rum

Caipiruva
(green drink with crushed red grapes)

Crushed red grapes
Raw sugar
Limes
Cachaca (Brazilian sugarcane rum)

Berry Bellini
(pinkish champagne cocktail)

Chambord Liqueur
Peach Schnaps
Champagne

Mojito Rosa
(sehr beliebter Cocktail – rot mit gehackten
Minzblättern)

1 TL frisches Himbeermark
6–7 Zweige gehackte Minze
1 TL Rohzucker
Eine ganze Limette in Scheiben geschnitten
6 cl Rum

Caipiruva
(grüner Cocktail mit gehackten roten
Trauben)

Gehackte rote Trauben
Rohzucker
Limetten
Cachaca (brasilianischer Rohrzuckerrum)

Berry Bellini
(pinkfarbener Champagnercocktail)

Chambord-Likör
Pfirsichgeist
Champagner

Mojito Rose
(boisson très populaire – rouge avec menthe verte pilée)

1 c. à café purée de framboises fraîches
6–7 rameaux menthe pilée
1 c. à café sucre de canne
Couper un citron vert en tranches
6 cl rhum

Caipiruva
(boisson verte avec des raisins rouges
écrasés

Raisins rouges écrasés
Sucre de canne
Citrons verts
Cachaca (rhum brésilien de sucre de canne)

Berry Bellini
(Cocktail au champagne rosé)

Liqueur de Chambord
Eau de vie de pêches
Champagne

Mojito Rosa
(es la bebida más popular – roja con hojas
de menta machacadas)

1 cucharadita puré de frambuesa fresca
6–7 ramitas de menta
1 cucharadita azúcar moreno
Una lima entera cortada en rodajas
6 cl ron

Caipiruva
(bebida verde con uvas rojas exprimidas)

Uvas rojas exprimidas
Azúcar moreno
Limas
Cachasa (ron brasileño de caña de azúcar)

Berry Bellini

Licor Chambord
Aguardiente de melocotón
Champán

Hue

Architect: Karim Amatullah with furniture by Maurice Villency |
Chef: Junnajet Hurapan (Jett)

91 Charles Street | New York, NY 10014
Phone: +1 212 691 4170
Subway: 1 and 9 to Christopher Street
Opening hours: Mon–Sun 11:30 am to 4 pm; Sun–Wed 6 pm to midnight,
Thu–Fri 6 pm to 12:30 am, Sat 6 pm to 1 am
Average price: $15
Cuisine: French-Vietnamese, Sushi Bar

Sushi Platter

Sushi-Platte
Plat de sushi
Tabla de sushi

Ahi tuna • salmon • sweet prawn • hamachi (yellow tail)

Served with fresh wasabi, ginger, and Japanese mountain peach.

Ahi-Tunfisch • Lachs • Süßgarnele • Hamachi (Gelbschwanzmakrele)

Serviert mit frischem Wasabi-Senf, Ingwer und japanischem Bergpfirsich.

Thon Ahi • saumon • crevettes sucrées • hamachi (limande à queue jaune)

Servi avec du wasabi frais, du gingembre et des pêches de la montagne japonaise.

Atún ahi • salmón • gamba dulce • hamachi (cola amarilla)

Servido con wasabi fresco, jengibre y melocotón japonés de la montaña.

Indochine

Architect: Aero Studios | Chef: Huy Chi Le

INSTITUTE

430 Lafayette Street | New York, NY 10003
Phone: +1 212 505 5111
Subway: 6 to Astor Place
Opening hours: Sun–Thu 5 pm to 12:30 am, Fri–Sat 5:30 pm to 12:30 am
Average price: Appetizers: $6 – $12.50, Entrees: $15.50 – $21
Cuisine: Asian, French Vietnamese

Vietnamese

Bouillabaisse

Fischsuppe nach Vietnamesischer Art
Bouillabaisse vietnamienne
Sopa de pescado vietnamita

Seafood:
2 dozen fresh cleaned mussels • 12 shelled and deveined large prawns • 1 cup calamari rings • 1/2 lb medium scallops

Vegetables:
2 cups finely shredded chinese cabbage • 1/2 cup fried minced shallots • 4 sprigs asian basil (for garnish) • 4 lime wedges (optional)

Broth:
4 cups pre-made fish broth (chicken broth can work, too) • 2 cups coconut milk • 2 tbsp finely shredded kaffir lime leaves • 1/2 tbsp shrimp paste • 2 tbsp garlic chili paste (adjust more or less to taste) • 1/2 tbsp curry powder (or paste) • 5 tbsp undiluted vietnamese fish sauce • 4 tbsp tomato paste • 1 tbsp sugar

Bring the fish broth, coconut milk, shrimp paste, chili paste, fish sauce, tomato paste, and sugar to a boil. Reduce heat. Add the curry powder and lime leaves. Simmer at medium heat for 10 minutes. Taste and adjust seasoning if necessary.

Add the mussels and let simmer for 2 or 3 minutes. Add the rest of the seafood and simmer at low heat for 2 minutes (don't overcook or else, the seafood will get tough and rubbery).

Divide the shredded cabbage in 4 fairly large bowls. Divide the seafood in the four bowls and pour the broth on top. Garnish with a sprig of basil and sprinkle fried shallots on top. Garnish with lime wedges.

Meeresfrüchte:
2 Dutzend frische, gesäuberte Miesmuscheln • 12 geschälte und ausgenommene Garnelen • 1 Tasse Tintenfischringe • 225 g mittelgroße Jakobsmuscheln

Gemüse:
2 Tassen fein gehackter Chinakohl • 1/2 Tasse frittierte gehackte Schalotten • 4 Zweige asiatisches Basilikum (zur Garnierung) • 4 Limettenscheiben (nach Belieben)

Brühe:
4 Tassen vorgekochte Fischbrühe (Hühnerbrühe geht auch) • 2 Tassen Kokosnussmilch • 2 EL fein gehackte Kaffir-Limettenblätter • 1/2 EL Krabbenpaste • 2 EL Knoblauch-Chili-Paste (je nach Geschmack) • 1/2 EL Currypulver (oder -Paste) • 5 EL unverdünnte vietnamesische Fischsauce • 4 EL Tomatenmark • 1 EL Zucker

Fischbrühe, Kokosnussmilch, Krabbenpaste, Chilipaste, Fischsauce, Tomatenmark und Zucker aufkochen. Hitze reduzieren. Currypulver und Limettenblätter dazugeben. Bei mittlerer Hitze 10 Minuten lang köcheln lassen. Abschmecken und falls nötig nachwürzen.

Die Muscheln hinzugeben und 2 bis 3 Minuten köcheln lassen. Die restlichen Meeresfrüchte hinzugeben und bei schwacher Hitze für 2 Minuten köcheln lassen (nicht zu lange kochen lassen, da die Meeresfrüchte sonst weich werden).

Den Chinakohl auf 4 große Suppenschüsseln verteilen. Meeresfrüchte in die Schüsseln geben und Brühe darüber gießen. Mit Basilikum und den frittierten Schalotten garnieren. Mit Limettenscheiben servieren.

Fruits de mer :
2 douzaines de moules fraîches nettoyées •
12 gambas décortiquées et nettoyées • 1
tasse de rondelles de calamars • 225 g de
noix de St Jacques moyennes

Légumes :
2 tasses de chou chinois coupé en fines
lamelles • 1/2 de tasse d'échalotes
hachées grillées • 4 bruns de basilic d'Asie
(garniture) • 4 quartiers de citron vert (au
choix)

Bouillon :
4 tasses de court-bouillon de poisson déjà
prêt (on peut aussi utiliser du bouillon de
poule) • 2 tasses de lait de noix de coco •
2 c. à soupe de feuilles de citron kaffir finement hachées • 1/2 c. à soupe de concentré de crevettes • 2 c. à soupe de concentré de chili à l'ail (ajoutez plus ou moins
pour donner du goût) • 1/2 c. à soupe de
poudre de curry • 5 c. à soupe de sauce de
poisson vietnamienne non diluée • 4 c. à
soupe de concentré de tomate • 1 c. à
soupe de sucre.

Amenez à ébullition le court-bouillon de
poisson, le lait de noix de coco, le concentré de crevettes, le concentré de chili, la
sauce de poisson, le concentré de tomate
et le sucre. Réduisez la chaleur. Ajoutez la
poudre de curry et les feuilles de citron kaffir. Laissez frémir à température moyenne
pendant 10 minutes. Goûtez et assaisonnez
davantage si nécessaire.

Ajoutez les moules et laissez frémir pendant 2 ou 3 minutes. Ajoutez le reste des
fruits de mer et laissez frémir à petit feu
pendant 2 minutes (ne cuisez pas trop
longtemps, sinon les fruits de mer risquent
d'être durs et caoutchouteux).

Partagez le chou émincé dans 4 bols assez
grands. Répartissez les fruits de mer sur
les bols et versez le bouillon par dessus.
Garnissez avec un brun de basilic et épar-
pillez les échalotes frites au-dessus.
Garnissez de quartiers de citron vert.

Marisco:
2 docenas de mejillones frescos limpios •
12 langostinos pelados • 1 taza de anillos
de calamar • 225 g de vieiras medianas

Vegetales:
2 tazas de col china cortada en juliana •
1/2 taza de cebolletas troceadas y fritas •
4 ramilletes de albahaca de Asia para decoración • 4 limas cortadas (opcional)

Caldo:
4 tazas de caldo de pescado (también
puede ser de pollo) • 2 tazas de leche de
coco • 2 cucharadas de hojas de lima cortada en juliana • 1/2 cucharada de pasta
de gambas • 2 cucharadas de pasta de ajo
con chiles (añadir al gusto) • 5 cucharadas
de pasta de pescado vietnamita • 4 cucharadas de pasta de tomate • 1/2 cucharada
de curry (o pasta de curry) • 1 cucharada
de azúcar.

Verter en el caldo la leche de coco, la
pasta de gambas, la de ajo con chiles, la
de pescado y la de tomate, el azúcar y llevar a ebullición. Bajar el fuego y añadir el
curry y las hojas de lima. Cocer a fuego
medio durante 10 minutos. Rectificar el
condimento si es necesario.

Agregar los mejillones y cocer a fuego lento
durante 2 o 3 minutos. Añadir el resto del
marisco y continuar la cocción a fuego lento
durante 2 minutos (no lo hay que dejarlo
demasiado para evitar que el marisco quede
duro y gomoso).

Repartir la col en cuatro grandes cuencos
junto al marisco y vertir el caldo por encima. Decorar con la albahaca y la cebolleta
frita. Emplear las hojas de lima para el
toque final.

Jefferson Restaurant

Architect: Philip Wu | Chef: Simpson Wong

121 West 10th Street | New York, NY 10011
Phone: +1 212 255 3333
Subway: A, C, E, F, V to West 4th Street
Opening hours: Mon–Thu 5:30 pm to 11 pm, Fri until 11:30 pm, Sat 11:30 am to 2:30 pm, 5:30 pm to 11:30 pm
Average price: Moderate to expensive, approximately, $50 per person for a three course meal, not including drinks
Cuisine: New American

Fig-Stuffed Quail

with Jicama Pancakes

Feigengefüllte Wachtel an Jicama-Pfannkuchen
Cailles farcies aux figues accompagnées de crêpes de jicama
Codorniz rellena de higos, con tortas de jícama

1 tsp finely chopped shallots • 2 quarts chicken stock • 1 cup clementine juice • 1 cup plum wine • 1 cup all-purpose flour • 1/2 cup corn starch • 1 cup julienned jicama • 1/2 cup finely chopped scallion • 1 cup water • salt and pepper to taste • 3 cups canola oil for frying • 4 quails • 2 black mission figs (dried figs can be substituted) • 2 tbsp extra virgin olive oil • 2 tbsp butter • 1 cup sliced oyster mushrooms • 1 pinch freshly ground cumin • 1 tbsp finely chopped chives

For the clementine plum wine sauce:
Place the chopped shallots, chicken stock, clementine juice, and plum wine in a sauce pan on medium heat and reduce heat until 1/4 the original volume. The sauce should have the consistency of a loose syrup. Reserve.

For the jicama pancake:
Combine the flour, corn starch, jicama, scallion and water in a bowl, and season with salt and pepper. Pour canola oil into a deep sauce pan and heat to 275 °F. Drop the pancake batter into the hot oil one dollop at a time, and fry each pancake for about 2 minutes until golden brown.

For the quails:
Season the quails with salt and pepper. Cut figs into halves and stuff one piece into each of the quails. Place a saute pan on medium-high heat and pour in olive oil. Place quails into pan, and saute for 2 minutes. Flip the quails over and place in a preheated 400 °F oven for another 2–3 minutes.

Heat 1 tbsp of butter in a separate pan and saute the oyster mushrooms. Season with salt and pepper and cook until tender and cooked through. Heat the clementine plum wine sauce on low heat and add the remaining 1 tbsp of butter and the cumin. Season with salt and pepper.

1 TL fein gehackte Schalotten • 2 l Hühnerbrühe • 1 Tasse Mandarinensaft • 1 Tasse Pflaumenwein • 1 Tasse Mehl • 1/2 Tasse Maisstärke • 1 Tasse gehackte Jicama • 1/2 Tasse fein gehackte Zwiebel • 1 Tasse Wasser • Salz und Pfeffer nach Geschmack • 3 Tassen Öl zum Braten • 4 Wachteln • 2 frische Feigen (können durch getrocknete ersetzt werden) • 2 EL kaltgepresstes Olivenöl • 2 EL Butter • 1 Tasse Austernpilze, in Scheiben geschnitten • 1 Prise frisch gemahlener Kreuzkümmel • 1 EL fein gehackter Schnittlauch

Für die Mandarinen-Pflaumenwein-Soße:
Die gehackten Zwiebeln, die Hühnerbrühe, den Mandarinensaft und den Pflaumenwein in eine kleine Pfanne auf mittlerer Hitze auf ein Viertel reduzieren. Die Soße sollte die Konsistenz eines zarten Sirups bekommen. Beiseite stellen.

Für die Jicama-Pfannkuchen:
Mehl, Stärke, Jicama, Zwiebel und Wasser in einer Schüssel verrühren, salzen und pfeffern. Das Bratöl in eine tiefe Sauciere geben und bei 135 °C Grad erhitzen. Den Pfannkuchenteig in das heiße Öl geben, nicht mehr als eine Kelle auf einmal, und jeden Pfannkuchen in etwa 2 Minuten goldbraun ausbacken.

Für die Wachteln:
Die Wachteln salzen und pfeffern. Die Feigen halbieren und jeweils eine Hälfte in eine Wachtel stecken. Eine kleine Pfanne auf mittlere Hitze stellen und Olivenöl hineinlaufen lassen. Die Wachteln anbraten und 2 Minuten anbraten. Die Wachteln umdrehen und in dem auf 200 °C vorgeheizten Ofen 2–3 Minuten weitergaren.

Einen EL Butter in einer weiteren Pfanne erhitzen und die Austernpilze darin anbraten. Mit Salz und Pfeffer würzen und langsam durchbraten. Die Mandarinen-Pflaumenwein-Soße langsam erhitzen und den restlichen EL Butter und den Kreuzkümmel hinzugeben. Mit Salz und Pfeffer abschmecken.

1 c. à café d'échalotes finement hachées • 2 l de bouillon de poule • 1 tasse de jus de clémentine • 1 tasse d'alcool de prune • 1 tasse de farine • 1/2 tasse de maïzena • 1 tasse de julienne de jicama (navet mexicain) • 1/2 tasse d'échalotes finement hachées • 1 tasse d'eau, sel et poivre pour donner du goût • 3 tasses d'huile à frire • 4 cailles • 2 figues noires (ou figues séchées) • 2 c. à soupe d'huile d'olive extra vierge • 2 c. à soupe de beurre • 1 tasse de pleurotes hachés • 1 pincée de cumin fraîchement moulu • 1 c. à soupe de ciboulette hachée fin

Pour la sauce au alcool de prune et clémentine :
Mettez dans une casserole les échalotes hachées, le bouillon de poule, le jus de clémentine, et alcool de prune dans une casserole à feu moyen et faites réduire jusqu'à 1/4 du volume initial. La sauce doit avoir la consistance d'un sirop léger. Réservez.

Pour les crêpes de Jicama :
Mélangez la farine, la maïzena, le jicama, les échalotes et l'eau dans un bol et assaisonnez de sel et poivre. Versez l'huile de canola dans une poêle à fond profond et chauffez à 135 °C . Versez la pâte à crêpe dans l'huile brûlante, louche après louche et cuire chaque crêpe pendant environ 2 minutes jusqu'à ce qu'elle soit bien dorée.

Pour les cailles :
Salez et poivrez les cailles. Coupez les figues en deux et farcissez chaque caille avec une figue. Chauffez une poêle à feu vif et versez-y de l'huile d'olive. Mettez les cailles dans la poêle et faites sauter 2 minutes Retournez les cailles et mettez les dans un four préchauffé à 200 °C pendant 2–3 minutes jusqu'au degré de cuisson désiré.

Chauffez une c. à soupe de beurre dans une poêle séparée et faites sauter les pleurotes. Salez et poivrez et laissez cuire afin qu'ils soient tendres et bien cuits. Chauffez la sauce au alcool de prune et clémentine à feu doux et ajoutez-y la c. à soupe de beurre restante et le cumin. Salez et poivrez.

1 cucharadita de cebolletas finamente picadas • 2 l de caldo de pollo • 1 taza de zumo de clementina • 1 taza de harina • 1/2 taza de fécula de maíz • 1 taza de jícama en rodajas • 1/2 taza de cebolla finamente picada • 1 taza de agua salpimentada • 3 tazas de aceite de girasol • 4 codornices • 2 higos secos • 2 cucharadas de aceite de oliva virgen • 2 cucharadas de mantequilla • 1 taza de setas picadas •1 pizca de comino recién picado • una cucharada de cebollinos finamente picados

Para la salsa de vino de ciruelas con clementina: Colocar los chalotes, el caldo de pollo, el zumo de clementina y el vino de ciruela en una sartén a fuego medio y llevar a ebullición para reducir hasta un 1/4 del volumen original. La salsa debería tener la consistencia de un jarabe ligero. Reservar.

Para las tortas de jícama:
Mezclar la harina, la fécula de maíz, la jícama, la cebolla y el agua en un cuenco, y salpimentar. Vertir el aceite de girasol en una sartén profunda y calentar a 135 °C. Colocar la masa de la torta en el aceite caliente, y freír cada torta durante 2 minutos hasta que quede dorada.

Para las codornices:
Salpimentar las codornices. Partir los higos por la mitad e introducir cada pedazo en cada una de las codornices. Calentar una sartén a fuego medio y vertir el aceite de oliva. Colocar las codornices en la sartén boca abajo, y saltear durante 2 minutos. Girarlas y poner las cuatro piezas en el horno, precalentado a 200 °C, durante 2 o 3 minutos más.

Entretanto, calentar una cucharada de mantequilla en una sartén y freír las setas. Salpimentar y cocinar hasta que estén hechas. Calentar la salsa de vino de ciruela a fuego lento y añadir el resto de la mantequilla y el comino. Salpimentar.

JoJo's

Architect: Diller & Scofidio | Jean-Georges Vongerichten |
Chef: Ron Gallo

160 East 64th Street | New York, NY 10021
Phone: +1 212 223 5656
www.jean-george.com
Subway: 4, 5, 6 to 58th and 2nd Street
Opening hours: Breakfast Mon–Fri 8 am to noon, Lunch Mon–Fri noon to
5 pm, Brunch Sat–Sun 10 am to 5 pm, Dinner Daily 6 pm to 2 am
Average price: Breakfast items $2 – $9, Appetizers $6 – $8, Entrées $8 – $16
Cuisine: French creative

Roasted Beet Salad

With Goat Cheese Fondue

Gebratene Beete-Salat mit Ziegenkäsefondue
Salade de betteraves rôties aux fondue de fromage de chèvre
Ensalada de remolacha asada con fondue de queso de cabra

Beets
Wash red and yellow beets. Toss separately with salt, olive oil and thyme and wrap separately in aluminium foil. Roast in hot oven until tender when pierced. Wear gloves and peel by rubbing skin off with a clean towel. When cool, cut in 1/2, then 1/8's.

Honey mustard
1/2 qt honey • 1/2 qt dijon • 3/4 qt sherry vinegar • 3/4 qt grapeseed oil • 1/4 qt olive oil • salt to taste

Mix honey and mustard and season with salt. Whisk in vinegar then emulsify with oils. Adjust seasoning. Toss walnuts with salt, white pepper and olive oil and bake on a sheet tray in a 350 °F oven until golden.

Goat cheese fondue
4 tbsp minced shallots • 1 tbsp butter • 1 qt cream • 2 logs goat cheese

Sweat shallots in foamy butter until translucent. Add cream and reduce to nape. Mount with the goat cheese and strain through the chinois. Season with salt and pepper. Keep warm in bain-marie.

To serve: Endive spears • red grapes washed and 1/2'd • chiffonade sage

In separate bowls toss 3 wedges of each beet with a little sage, salt and the honey mustard. Arrange on the left side of a rectangle plate. In the middle put a little cup with the goat cheese fondue. On the right arrange 3 spears of the endive which has been tossed with the honey mustard and toss some walnuts and grapes on top and around.

Beete
Rote und gelbe Beete waschen. Einzeln mit Salz, Olivenöl und Thymian bestreuen und in Alufolie einwickeln. Im heißen Ofen braten, bis sie gar sind. Probe durch Einstechen machen. Küchenhandschuhe anziehen und Gemüsehaut mit sauberem Küchentuch abreiben. Abgekühlte Beete erst halbieren, dann achteln.

Honigsenf
1/2 l Honig • 1/2 l Dijonsenf • 3/4 l Sherryessig • 3/4 l Traubenkernöl • 1/4 l Olivenöl • Salz nach Geschmack

Honig und Senf mischen und salzen. Mit Essig verquirlen und dann mit den Ölen verrühren. Abschmecken. Walnüsse mit Salz, weißem Pfeffer und Olivenöl bestreuen und auf dem Ofenblech bei 175 °C goldbraun braten.

Fondue aus Ziegenkäse
4 EL gehackte Schalotten • 1 EL Butter • 1 l Sahne • 2 Rollen Ziegenkäse

Schalotten in schaumiger Butter glasieren. Sahne dazugeben und reduzieren. Mit Ziegenkäse verrühren und durch Trichtersieb laufen lassen. Mit Salz und Pfeffer abschmecken. Im Wasserbad warm halten.

Servieren: Endivienspieße • gewaschene und halbierte rote Trauben • dünn geschnittene Salbeistreifen

Je 3 Scheiben von jeder Beete mit etwas Salbei, Salz und dem Honigsenf in separaten Schüsseln anrichten. Schüsseln auf die linke Seite eines rechteckigen Tellers stellen. In die Mitte des Tellers eine kleine Tasse mit dem Fondue aus Ziegenkäse stellen. Rechts 3 Endivienspieße anrichten, die mit dem Honigsenf bestrichen sind. Rundherum mit Walnüssen und Trauben garnieren.

Betteraves

Lavez les betteraves rouges et jaunes. Assaisonnez chacune de sel, huile d'olive et thym et enveloppez séparément dans de l'aluminium. Rôtir au four jusqu'à ce qu'elles soient tendres si on les perce. Avec des gants frottez la peau avec un torchon propre. Une fois refroidies, coupez-les en 2 et en 8.

Moutarde au miel

1/2 l de miel • 1/2 l moutarde de Dijon • 3/4 l de vinaigre de Sherry • 3/4 l de graines de raisin • 1/4 l d'huile d'olive • sel

Mélangez miel et moutarde et salez. Fouettez le vinaigre et émulsifiez avec l'huile. Ajoutez l'assaisonnement. Saupoudrez les noix de sel, poivre blanc et huile d'olive et mettez au four, sur une plaque, à 175 °C et laissez dorer.

Fondue de fromage de chèvre

4 c. à soupe d'échalotes émincées • 1 c. à soupe de beurre • 1 l de crème • 2 bûches de fromage de chèvre

Faites suer les échalotes dans du beurre mousseux pour qu'elles deviennent transparentes. Ajoutez la crème et réduire pour napper. Fouettez avec le fromage de chèvre et passez au chinois. Salez, poivrez. Gardez chaud au bain-marie.

Servir : Feuilles d'endives • raisins rouges lavés • chiffonnade de sauge

Dans des bols séparés, placez trois quartiers de chaque betterave avec sauge, sel et moutarde au miel. Arrangez à gauche sur une assiette rectangulaire. Mettez au centre une petite tasse de fondue de fromage de chèvre. A droite, décorez avec trois feuilles d'endive enduites de moutarde au miel et jetez quelques noix et grains de raisin au-dessus et autour.

Remolacha

Lavar y pelar remolachas rojas y amarillas; frotarlas con sal, aceite de oliva y tomillo, y envolverlas separadamente en papel de aluminio. Asar al horno hasta que estén tiernas al pincharlas. Una vez protegidas las manos con guantes, pelarlas arrastrando la piel con un trapo limpio. Cuando estén frías, cortarlas en ocho trozos iguales.

Mostaza de miel

1/2 l miel • 1/2 l de mostaza Dijon • 3/4 l de vinagre • 200 g de nueces • 1/4 l de aceite de oliva • sal al gusto

Mezclar la miel y la mostaza y sazonar. Batir con el vinagre y agregar el aceite. Rectificar de sal. Mezclar las nueces con sal, pimienta blanca y aceite de oliva y tostarlas en una bandeja en el horno a 175 °C hasta que se doren.

Fondue de queso de cabra

4 cucharadas de ajo picado • una cuchara da de mantequilla • 1 l nata • 2 trozos de queso de cabra

Rehogar el ajo en mantequilla hasta que quede transparente. Añadir la nata y reducirla. Mezclar con el queso de cabra y pasarlo por el pasapurés. Sazona y mantener caliente al baño María.

Para servir: Endibias • uvas rojas partidas por la mitad • salvia en juliana

En cuencos separados colocar un trozo de remolacha con una tira de verdura, sal y la mostaza de miel. Disponerlo en la parte izquierda de un plato rectangular. En el centro colocar una pequeña taza con la fondue, y a la derecha, tres hojas de endibia, cubierta de mostaza, nueces y uvas.

Lenox Lounge

Chef: Michael Wilson I Owner: Alvin Reed

288 Lenox Avenue I New York, NY 10027
Phone: + 1 212 427 0253
www.lenoxlounge.com
Subway: 2 and 3 to 125th Street
Opening hours: Daily noon to 4 am, Lunch Mon–Fri 11 am to 2 pm
Average price: Food $4 – $25, Drinks $3 – $20
Cuisine: Southern/Soul

Red Devil

1/2 oz vodka • 1/2 oz Southern Comfort • 1/2 oz banana liqueur • dash Triple Sec • dash Rose's lime juice • dash Sloe gin • dash Amaretto • dash grenadine • 3 oz orange juice

Shaken. Strain over Ice.

15 ml Wodka • 15 ml Southern Comfort • 15 ml Bananenlikör • Spritzer Triple Sec • Spritzer Rose's Limettensaft • Spritzer Sloe Gin • Spritzer Amaretto • Spritzer Grenadine • 90 ml Orangensaft

Geschüttelt und auf Eis servieren.

15 ml de Vodka • 15 ml de Southern Comfort • 15 ml de liqueur de banane • quelques gouttes de Triple Sec • quelques gouttes de jus de citron vert Rose • quelques gouttes de Sloe gin • quelques gouttes d'amaretto • quelques gouttes de grenadine • 90 ml de jus d'orange

Passez au shaker. Versez sur la glace.

15 ml de vodka • 15 ml de Southern Comfort (licor de whisky) • 15 ml de licor de banana • 1 chorro de Triple Sec (licor de naranja) • 1 chorro de zumo de lima • 1 chorro de ginebra Sloe • 1 chorro de Amaretto • 1 chorro de granadina • 90 ml de zumo de naranja

Agitar y servir con hielo.

Lever House

Architect: John Mc Donald & Joshua Pickard |
Chef: Dan Silverman

390 Park Avenue/53rd Street | New York, NY 10022
Phone: +1 212 888 2700
www.leverhouse.com, info@leverhouse.com
Subway: E, V to Lexington Avenue/53rd Street, 6 to 51st Street
Opening hours: Mon–Thu 5:30 pm to 11 pm, Fri–Sat 5:30 pm to 11:30 pm,
Sun 5:30 to 10 pm
Average price: from $17
Cuisine: Country Club inspired American

Piggy Brine

Pökellake zum Einlegen von Schweinekoteletts
Marinade à la Piggy
Salmuera para carne de cerdo

15 cups water • 18 tbsp sugar • 9 tbsp sea salt • fresh bay leaves • juniper • garlic cloves • red pepper flakes

Combine all and dissolve salt and sugar, brine pork chops overnight.

Piggy spice mix
1/2 tbsp allspice • 2 tbsp coriander seed • 1/2 tsp cumin seed • 1 tbsp juniper berries • 1 tsp black pepper

Combine all, toast till fragrant and grind medium fine.

Piggy apple sauce with pomegranate molasses
1 1/2 cups organic apple juice • 2 cardamom pods • 1 cinnamon stick • 2 apples, cut, cored but not peeled • 2 tbsp pomegranate molasses

Combine juice, cardamom, cinnamon and salt, boil to reduce by 1/2. Add apple pieces and simmer covered for about 1/2 hour and pass through a food mill.

Sweet potato boulangere
Spanish onions, peeled and sliced thin • sweet potatoes, peeled and sliced on the meat slicer • aleppo pepper • thyme sprigs and bay leaves • chicken stock • salt and pepper

Sweat onions in butter over medium heat, seasoning well with salt, freshly ground black pepper, aleppo and bay leaves. Cook covered until the onions are soft and liquid has rendered. Strain onions through a perforated pan and reserve the liquid. In a hotel pan layer onions and sweet potato slices, making four layers in total, finishing with sweet potatoes. Combine equal quantities onion cooking liquid and chicken stock, bring to a boil and pour over and around sweet potatoes. Liquid should come to the level of the gratin top. Dot the gratin with butter and place thyme sprigs over the top. Cover with foil and bake in a preheated 350 °F oven until the sweet potatoes are cooked through. Uncover the gratin and bake until the top is lightly caramelized.

15 Tassen Wasser • 18 EL Zucker • 9 EL Meersalz • frische Lorbeerblätter • Wacholder • Knoblauch-Gewürznelken • Paprika

Verrühren, Salz und Zucker auflösen, Schweinekoteletts über Nacht in Pökellake einlegen.

Gewürzmischung für Schweinefleisch
1/2 EL Piment • 2 EL Koriandersamen • 1/2 TL Kreuzkümmel • 1 EL Wacholderbeeren • 1 TL schwarzer Pfeffer

Alle Gewürze gut mischen, rösten, bis sie Aroma freigeben, und dann mittelfein mahlen.

Apfelsauce mit Granatapfelsirup
1 1/2 Tassen Bio-Apfelsaft • 2 Schoten Kardamom • 1 Zimtstange • 2 Äpfel, geschnitten, ohne Gehäuse, aber mit Schale • 2 EL Granatapfelsirup

Saft, Kardamom, Zimt und Salz vermischen, und auf die Hälfte einkochen lassen. Apfelstücke hinzufügen und abgedeckt etwa eine halbe Stunde köcheln lassen und dann durch eine Küchenmühle passieren.

Süßkartoffeln „Boulangere"
Spanische Zwiebeln, geschält und in dünne Scheiben geschnitten • Süßkartoffeln, geschält, mit der Fleischschneidemaschine geschnitten • Aleppopfeffer • Thymianzweige • Lorbeerblätter • Hühnerbrühe • Salz und Pfeffer

Zwiebeln in Butter bei mittlerer Hitze anschwitzen, mit Salz, frisch gemahlenem schwarzem Pfeffer und Lorbeerblättern würzen. Zudecken und kochen, bis die Zwiebeln weich sind und sich Saft gebildet hat. Zwiebel durch ein grobes Sieb passieren und Flüssigkeit beiseite stellen. In großer Auflaufform Zwiebeln und Süßkartoffelscheiben in vier Lagen übereinander schichten und mit einer Lage Kartoffeln abschließen. Zwiebelsud und Hühnerbrühe im gleichen Verhältnis mischen, aufkochen und über Kartoffeln gießen. Flüssigkeit sollte Auflaufform bis zum Rand füllen. Darauf Butter und Thymian geben. Mit Folie bedecken und im vorgeheizten Ofen bei 175 °C backen. Folie abnehmen, backen bis die Oberseite karamellisiert ist.

15 tasses d'eau • 18 c. à soupe de sucre • 9 c. à soupe de sel de mer • feuilles de laurier frais • genièvre • gousses d'ail • pointes de piment rouge

Mélangez les ingrédients et dissoudre sel et sucre. Faites mariner les côtes toute la nuit.

Mélange d'épices à la Piggy
1/2 c. à soupe de quatre épices• 2 c. à soupe de graines de coriandre • 1/2 c. à café de graines de cumin • 1 c. à soupe de baies de genièvre • 1 c. à café de poivre

Mélangez le tout, grillez jusqu'à ce que les parfums se développent. Moudre assez fin.

Compote de pomme à la Piggy accompagnée de mélasse de grenade
1 1/2 tasses jus de pomme biologique • 2 gousses cardamome • 1 bâton cannelle • 2 pommes, coupées, épépinées mais non pelées • 2 c. à soupe de mélasse de grenade

Mélangez le jus, la cardamome, la cannelle et le sel et portez à ébullition. Réduire de moitié. Ajoutez les morceaux de pomme, couvrez et laissez frémir pendant environ 1/2 heure. Passez au chinois.

Patate douce boulangère
Gros oignons d'Espagne • patates douces pelées et passées au hachoir à viande • poivre d'Aleph • brins de thym • feuilles de laurier • bouillon de poule • sel et poivre

Faites suer les oignons dans du beurre à feu moyen, assaisonnez avec poivre noir fraîchement moulu, poivre d'Aleph et feuilles de laurier. Couvrez et faites cuire à feu doux jusqu'à ce que les oignons soient tendres et qu'ils aient rendu tout leur jus. Mettez-les dans une passoire et réservez le jus. Dans un plat à gratin, alternez une couche d'oignons et de patates douces pour faire en tout quatre couches. Ajoutez du beurre et des brins de thym sur le gratin. Disposez dans le four préchauffé à 180 °C jusqu'à ce que les patates douces soient parfaitement cuites. Découvrez le gratin et continuez la cuisson pour caraméliser.

15 tazas de agua • 18 cucharadas de azúcar • 9 cucharadas de sal de mar • hojas de baya frescas • enebro • dientes de ajo • pimientos rojos desmenuzados

Mezclar todos los ingredientes y disolver la sal y el azúcar. Macerar la carne de cerdo en esta salmuera durante toda la noche.

Mezcla picante para carne de cerdo
1/2 cucharada de pimienta • 2 cucharadas de semilla de cilantro • 1/2 cucharada de semilla de comino • 1 cucharada de bayas de enebro • 1 cucharada de pimienta negra

Mezclar todos los ingredientes y machacar las especias hasta obtener un polvo no demasiado fino.

Salsa de manzana con melaza de granada para carne de cerdo • 1 1/2 tazas de zumo de manzana natural • 2 vainas de cardamomo • 1 bastón de canela • 2 manzanas cortadas (sin el corazón pero con la piel) • 2 cucharadas de melaza de granada

Mezcle el zumo, el cardamomo, la canela y la sal, y llevar a ebullición hasta reducirlo a la mitad. Añadir los trozos de manzana y cocer durante media hora.Triturar con un pasapurés.

Patatas dulces a la panadera
cebollas finamente picadas • patatas dulces, peladas y picadas con la picadora de carne • pimienta negra en grano • un ramillete de tomillo • hojas de baya • caldo de pollo • sal y pimienta

Rehogar las cebollas en mantequilla a fuego medio y sazonar con sal, pimienta negra recién picada y las hojas de baya. Cocer tapado hasta que las cebollas queden blandas. Colar la cebolla y reservar el preparado. Disponer alternadamente en una fuente cuatro capas de cebolla y patatas dulces. Untar con mantequilla la parte superior y añadir el tomillo. Introducir en el horno precalentado a 180 °C hasta que las patatas dulces estén cocinadas. Gratinar para que la parte superior quede caramelizada.

Matsuri

Architect: Sean MacPherson and Eric Goode in collaboration with Mikio Shinagawa | Chef: Tadashi Ono

363 W. 16th Street (Maritime Hotel) | New York, NY 10011
Phone: +1 212 243 6400
Subway: A, C, E to 14th Street
Opening hours: Sun–Wed 6 pm to 1:30 am, Thu–Sat 6 pm to 2:30 am
Average price: $11 – $22
Cuisine: Japanese

Matsuri's Sushi

and Sashimi

Matsuris Sushi und Sashimi
Sushi et Sashimi de Matsuri
Sushi y Sashimi de Matsuri

Sushi
2 p. tuna • 2 p. yellowtail • 2 p. salmon •
2 p. scallops • 2 p. tobiko • 2 p. eel • 2 p.
egg • 2 p. shrimp • 2 p. white fish

Sashimi
8 p. tuna • 6 p. yellow tail • 4 p. salmon •
4 p. white fish • 2 p. ikura • 2 p. cucumber

Sushi
2 Portionen Tunfisch • 2 Portionen
Gelbschwanzmakrele • 2 Portionen Lachs •
2 Portionen Jakobsmuschel • 2 Portionen
Tobiko • 2 Portionen Aal • 2 Portionen
Omelette • 2 Garnelen • 2 Portionen
Weißfisch

Sashimi
8 Portionen Tunfisch • 6 Portionen
Gelbschwanzmakrele • 4 Portionen Lachs •
4 Portionen Weißfisch • 2 Portionen Ikura •
2 Portionen mit Gurke

Sushi
2 morceaux de thon • 2 morceaux de
limande à queue jaune • 2 morceaux de
saumon • 2 morceaux de noix de St
Jacques • 2 morceaux de Tobiko • 2 morceaux d'anguille • 2 morceaux d'omelette •
2 crevettes • 2 morceaux de poisson blanc

Sashimi
8 morceaux de thon • 6 morceaux de
limande à queue jaune • 4 morceaux de
saumon • 4 morceaux de poisson blanc •
2 morceaux d'Ikura • 2 morceaux de
concombre

Sushi
2 trozos de atún • 2 trozos de jurel • 2 trozos de salmón • 2 vieiras • 2 trozos de
tobiko • 2 trozos de anguila • 2 trozos de
tortilla • 2 gambas • 2 trozos de merluza

Sashimi
8 trozos de atún • 6 trozos de jurel • 4 trozos de salmón • 4 trozos de merluza • 2
trozos de ikura • 2 trozos de pepino

McDonald's

Architect: Charles Morris Mount

220 West 42nd Street | New York, NY 10036
Phone: +1 212 840 6250
www.mcdonalds.com
Subway: 1, 2, 3, 7, 9, E, C, A, S, R, N, W to 42nd Street Times Square
Opening hours: Mon–Sat 6 am to 2 am, Sun 7 am to 2 am
Average price: $4 – $7
Cuisine: Fast Food

Meet

Architect: Kushner studios I Chef: Patrik Landberg

71-73 Gansevoort Street (West Village) I New York, NY 10014
Phone: +1 212 242 0990
www.the-meet.com
Subway: A, C, E to 14th Street, L to Eighth Avenue
Opening hours: Dinner Mon–Wed 6 pm to 23 pm, Thu–Sat until 23:30 pm I
Bar until 2 am
Average price: Appetizers $8 – $16, Entrées $18 – $32
Cuisine: American, Italian, Southern/Soul

Roasted Duck Breast
with Seville Orange Marmalade, Butternut Squash Puree

Gebratene Entenbrust mit Orangenmarmelade aus Sevilla
Butternuss-Kürbis-Püree

Magret de canard rôti avec confiture d'oranges de Séville,
purée de courge butternut

Pechuga de pato asada con mermelada de naranjas sevillanas,
puré de mantequilla de cacahuete

4 duck breasts • 2 cups duck stock • 1 cup red wine • 1/2 jalapeno pepper • 1 onion (red or spanish) • 1 cinnamon stick • zest from 1 orange (save the rest for the marmalade) • 1 cup brown sugar • 1/2 cup balsamic vinagrette

Sauce
Sautee onion, jalapeno, orange zest add in duck stock, red wine, cinnamon stick and balsamic. Reduce to 1/2, add brown sugar after taste, add salt and pepper.

Roast duck until golden brown, put in oven 350 °F for 5 minutes, rest 2 minutes (for medium meat temperature), slice into thin slices, drizzle sauce over.

Orange Marmalade
3 oranges and orange zest from sauce • 1 red onion • 1 cinnamon stick • 1 cup orange juice • 1/2 cup sugar • olive oil

Take out juice and files from oranges. Slice red onion, sautee in olive oil, add orange juice, orange zest and file of orange, cinnamon stick and sugar. Reduce for 45 minutes. Let cool for an hour.

Butternut squash puree
2 butternut squashs • 1 cup chicken stock • brown sugar • salt and pepper • brown sugar • olive oil • butter

Cut butternut squash in half, roast in oven for 50 minutes. Drizzle with salt, pepper and olive oil, let cool. Put squash (scoop out, throw away the skin), chicken stock and some butter in blender, add sugar for taste.

4 Entenbrüste • 2 Tassen Entenbrühe • 1 Tasse Rotwein • 1/2 Jalapeñopfeffer • 1 Zwiebel (rote oder spanische) • 1 Zimtstange • Schale von einer 1 Orange (Rest der Orange für die Marmelade aufheben) • 1 Tasse braunen Zucker • 1/2 Tasse Balsamico-Essig

Sauce
Zwiebeln, Jalapeño und Orangenschale anbraten und Entenbrühe, Rotwein, Zimtstange und Balsamico-Essig hinzufügen. Auf die Hälfte einkochen und Zucker dazugeben. Salzen und pfeffern.

Ente braten, bis sie schön goldbraun ist, für 5 Minuten bei 175 °C in den Ofen setzen. 2 Minuten abkühlen lassen, in Scheiben schneiden und mit Sauce begießen.

Orangenmarmelade
3 Orangen und Orangenschale von der Sauce • 1 rote Zwiebel • 1 Zimtstange • 1 Tasse Orangensaft • 1/2 Tasse Zucker • Olivenöl

Saft der Orangen auspressen und Fruchtfleisch herauslösen. Rote Zwiebel in Scheiben schneiden und in Olivenöl anbraten, Orangensaft, Orangenschale und Fruchtfleisch, Zimtstange und Zucker dazugeben und 45 Minuten einkochen lassen. Eine Stunde abkühlen lassen.

Butternuss-Kürbis-Püree
2 Butternuss-Kürbisse • 1 Tasse Hühnerbrühe • brauner Zucker • Salz und Pfeffer • Olivenöl • Butter

Kürbisse halbieren und 50 Minuten im Ofen backen. Mit Salz, Pfeffer, Olivenöl bestreichen, abkühlen lassen. Kürbismark, Hühnerbrühe und etwas Butter im Mixer zu Püree rühren, Zucker nach Belieben dazugeben.

4 magrets de canard • 2 tasses de bouillon
de canard • 1 tasse de vin rouge • 1/2
piment de jalapeño • 1 oignon (rouge ou
d'Espagne) • 1 bâton de cannelle • zeste
d'une orange (gardez le reste pour la confiture) • 1 tasse de sucre roux • 1/2 tasse
de vinaigre balsamique

Sauce
Faites revenir les oignons, le jalapeño, le
zeste d'orange, ajoutez au bouillon de
canard avec le vin rouge, la cannelle et le
vinaigre balsamique. Faites réduire de 1/2,
ajoutez le sucre roux, goûtez et ensuite
salez et poivrez.
Faites bien dorer le canard, et enfournez à
175 °C pendant 5 minutes. Laissez reposer
2 minutes (à temperature moyenne).
Coupez en tranches et couvrez de sauce.

Confiture d'orange
3 oranges et le zeste d'orange de la sauce •
1 oignon rouge • 1 bâton de cannelle • 1
verre de jus d'orange • 1/2 tasse de sucre •
huile d'olive

Enlevez le jus et les quartiers de l'orange.
Faites revenir les tranches d'oignon dans
l'huile d'olive, ajoutez le jus, le zeste et les
quartiers d'orange, le bâton de cannelle et
le sucre. Réduisez pendant 45 minutes.
Laissez refroidir une heure.

Puree de courge Butternut
2 courges butternut • 1 tasse de bouillon
de poule • sucre roux • sel et poivre •
huile d'olive • beurre

Coupez la courge butternut en deux et rôtir
au four pendant 50 minutes. Ajoutez sel,
poivre et huile d'olive et laissez refroidir.
Dans un mixer, mettez la chair de la courge
(jetez la peau), le bouillon de poule et un
peu de beurre et ajoutez du sucre au goût.

4 pechugas de pato • 2 tazas de caldo de
pato • 1 copa de vino tinto • 1/2 jalapeño •
1 cebolla • 1 ramita de canela • ralladura
de 1 naranja • 1 taza de azúcar moreno •
1/2 taza de vinagre

Salsa
Saltear la cebolla, el jalapeño, la ralladura
de naranja y agregar el caldo, el vino tinto,
la canela en rama y el vinagre. Reducir a la
mitad y añadir el azúcar moreno, la sal y la
pimienta.

Asar el pato hasta que esté dorado con el
horno a 175 °C durante 5 minutos y después bajar a fuego lento durante dos minutos
más; cubrir los filetes con la salsa.

Mermelada de naranja
3 naranjas y su ralladura • 1 cebolla roja •
1 ramita de canela • 1 taza de zumo de
naranja • 1/2 taza de azúcar • aceite de
oliva

Exprimir el zumo y cortar las naranjas.
Dorar las cebollas en una sartén con aceite
oliva, previamente cortadas en juliana.
Añadir el zumo de naranja, la ralladura, las
naranjas en pedacitos, la canela y el azúcar, y reducir durante 45 minutos. Dejar
enfriar durante 1 hora.

Puré de calabaza
2 calabazas • 1 taza de caldo de pollo •
azúcar moreno • sal y pimienta • aceite de
oliva • mantequilla

Partir las calabazas por la mitad y asarlas
al horno durante 50 minutos. Añadir la sal,
la pimienta, el aceite de oliva y dejar enfriar. Añadir el caldo de pollo y un poco de
azúcar.

Mercer Kitchen

Architect: Diller & Scofidio in collaboration with Jean-Georges Vongerichten I Chef: Christopher Beischer

The Mercer Hotel I 99 Prince Street I New York, NY 10012
Phone: +1 212 966 5454
Subway: N, R, W to Prince Street
Opening hours: Mon–Thu 7 am to midnight, Fri–Sat 7 am to 1 am, Sun 7 am to midnight
Average price: Appetizers $9 – 14, Entrees $16 – $27, Pizza $13 – 19
Cuisine: American Creative

Tuna Wasabi Pizza

Tunfisch-Wasabi-Pizza
Pizza au thon et wazzabi
Pizza de atún y wasabi

Pizza Dough
3 cups AP flour • 1 tsp salt, fine sea • 1 tbsp honey • 2 tbsp olive oil • 3/4 cup cold water • 1 pck yeast • 1/4 cup warm water

Place flour in a mixer with dough hook. Combine the salt, honey, olive oil and cold water in a bowl and mix well. Dissolve the yeast in the warm water and let proof for 10 minutes. With the motor running, slowly pour the salt and honey mixture in, then pour in the dissolved yeast. Process until the dough forms a ball. If it is sticky, add sprinklings of flour. Portion dough into 2 bowls. Let the dough rest overnight. Portion dough into 60 g pieces. Roll each piece into a smooth tight ball. Place on floured sheet pan, cover and refrigerate.

Wasabi cheese
6 portion cream cheese • 6 portion ricotta cheese • 18 oz Mirin • 1 1/2 cups rice wine vinegar • 1 1/2 cups white wine • 3 cups wasabi paste • 6 limes-juiced

Combine the cheeses in a mixer and blend until smooth. Add remaining ingredients and process until combined. Let sit overnight, and strain through a chinois.

Ponzu dipping sauce
1 cup mirin • 1 cup rice vinegar • 1/2 cup soy sauce—combine.

For service:
Tuna-grind seasoned with salt, pepper and olive oil. Weigh 2 1/2 oz portions and put between 2 layers of plastic wrap and flatten. Use a 16 cm ring mold to shape the tuna.

Pizzateig
3 Tassen Mehl • 1 TL feines Meersalz • 1 EL Honig • 2 EL Olivenöl • 3/4 Tasse kaltes Wasser • 1 Päckchen Hefe • 1/4 Tasse warmes Wasser

Mehl in Mixgerät mit Teigrührbesen geben. Salz, Honig, Olivenöl und kaltes Wasser zusammen in eine Schüssel geben und gut umrühren. Hefe in warmem Wasser auflösen und 10 Minuten gehen lassen. Bei laufendem Rührbesen die Salz- und Honigmischung zu dem Mehl mischen, dann die aufgelöste Hefe untermischen. Rühren, bis der Teig zu einer Kugel wird. Wenn der Teig klebt, noch etwas Mehl dazu geben. Teig auf zwei Schüsseln verteilen. Über Nacht aufgehen lassen. Teig in 60 g-Stücke teilen. Teigstück zu einem glatten Ball rollen. Auf mit Mehl bestäubtes Blech geben, abdecken und einfrieren.

Wasabi-Käse
6 Portionen Sahne-Käse • 6 Portion Ricotta-Käse • 540 g Mirin • 1 1/2 Tassen Reisweinessig • 1 1/2 Tassen Weißwein • 3 Tassen Wasabi-Paste • 6 ausgepresste Limetten

Käse in einen Mixer geben und vermischen, bis sich eine glatte Masse bildet. Restliche Zutaten hinzufügen und weiterrühren, bis alles vermischt ist. Über Nacht ruhen lassen und durch einen Küchentrichter passieren.

Ponzu-Dip
1 Tasse Mirin • 1 Tasse Reisessig • 1/2 Tasse Sojasauce – vermischen.

Zum Servieren:
Tunfisch-Streifen mit Salz, Pfeffer und Olivenöl gewürzt. Portionen von ca. 75 g abwiegen und zwischen 2 Schichten Plastikfolie legen und flach pressen. Mit einer Springform von 16 cm Durchmesser Tunfisch formen.

Pâte à pizza
3 tasses de farine • 1 c. à café de sel fin de mer • 1 c. à soupe de miel • 2 c. à soupe d'huile d'olive • 3/4 tasse d'eau froide • 1 paquet de levure • 1/4 tasse d'eau chaude

Mettez la farine dans le mixer avec les batteurs à pâte. Mélangez bien dans un bolle sel, le miel, l'huile d'olive et l'eau froide. Après avoir dissout la levure dans l'eau chaude, laissez la reposer 10 minutes. Fouettez et versez doucement le mélange sel et miel sur la levure dissoute. Mélangez jusqu'à obtention d'une boule. Si elle colle, ajoutez un peu de farine. Faites deux boules de pâte. Laissez reposer la pâte toute la nuit. Portionnez-la en part de 60 g chacune. Roulez chaque part en une boule serrée. Mettez sur un plateau fariné. Couvrez et mettez au réfrigérateur.

Fromage Wasabi
6 pots de fromage blanc • 6 pots de ricotta • 540 g de mirin • 1 1/2 tasses de vinaigre de vin de riz • 1 1/2 tasses de vin blanc • 3 tasses de crème de wasabi • le jus de 6 citrons verts

Mélangez les fromages dans un mixer jusqu'à obtention d'un mélange onctueux. Ajoutez les autres ingrédients et mélangez. Laissez reposer 1 nuit et passez au chinois.

Sauce Ponzu pour trempette
1 tasse de mirin • 1 tasse de vinaigre de riz • 1/2 tasse sauce soja – mélangez.

Pour servir :
Salez le thon en morceaux. Ajoutez poivre et huile d'olive. Pesez des portions de 75 g, placez entre deux films de plastique et aplatissez. Moulez le thon dans un plat.

Masa de la pizza
3 tazas de harina • una cucharadita de sal marina • 1 cucharada de miel • 2 cucharadas de aceite de oliva • 3/4 taza de agua fría • 1 paquete de levadura • 1/4 taza agua caliente

Colocar la harina en una mezcladora que disponga de accesorio para hacer masa. Mezclar bien la sal, la miel, el aceite y el agua fría en un cuenco. Disolver la levadura en agua caliente y dejar que repose durante 10 minutos. Con el motor en marcha, vertir lentamente la mezcla de sal y miel y añadir la levadura disuelta. Amasar hasta conseguir una bola. Si está pegajosa, espolvorear con harina. Separar la masa en dos partes y dejar reposar durante toda la noche. Cortar la masa en porciones de unos 60 g. Amasar y formar una bola suave y prieta con cada una. Colocar en una bandeja recubierta con harina e introducir en el refrigerador.

Queso wasabi
6 porciones de queso cremoso • 6 porciones de queso ricota • 570 g de mirin • 1 1/2 tazas de vinagre de arroz • 1 1/2 tazas de vino blanco • 3 tazas de pasta wasabi • zumo de 6 limas

Mezclar los quesos en la mezcladora y batir hasta que quede homogéneo. Añadir los ingredientes restantes y mezclar bien. Dejar reposar durante toda la noche y pasarlo por el pasapurés.

Salsa de dipping Ponzu
1 taza de mirin • 1 taza de vinagre de arroz • 1/2 taza de soja –mezclar.

Para servir:
Atún picado sazonado con sal, pimienta y aceite de oliva. Separar porciones de 75 g, colocarlas entre dos capas de envoltorio de plástico y aplástelas. Utilizar un molde redondo de 16 cm de diámetro para dar forma al atún.

Mix

Architect: Patrick Jouin | Chef: Dougoaf Pfaltis

68 West 58th Street (Midtown West) | New York, NY 10019
Phone: +1 212 583 0300
www.mixny.com
Subway: N, R, W to 5th Avenue
Opening hours: Lunch Mon–Fri 11:30 am to 2:30 pm, Dinner Daily 5:30 pm to 10:30 pm
Average price: Three-course tasting menu $72 unique price
Cuisine: American, French

Mix Chocolate Cake

Makes 6 individual cakes in cupcake tin or mold

Schokoladenkuchen. Für 6 einzelne Küchlein in Backförmchen
Gâteau au chocolat. 6 gâteaux individuels en caissette ou en moule
Pastel de chocolate. Para 6 personas en moldes individuales

Biscuit
90 g hazelnuts • 90 g confectioners sugar •
10 g flour • 120 g egg whites • 35 g sugar

Roast hazelnuts in the oven for about 8
minutes at 320 °F. When the nuts have
cooled, grind them into a fine powder. Add
the confectioners sugar and the flour to the
ground nuts. Beat the egg whites and sugar
to make a meringue. Combine the meringue
with the nut mixture stirring slowly by hand.
Bake in small circle tins at 320 °F for
approx. 15–20 minutes.

Praline Feuilletine
60 g praline Valrhona • 30 g feuilletine •
15 g chocolate milk Valrhona Jivara

Melt the chocolate in a bain marie. Add the
praline first. Then add the feuilletine and
stir thoroughly. Pour mixture onto a baking
sheet lined with parchment paper and
spread into a thin layer.

Chocolate Mousse
50 g milk • 2 egg yolks • 60 g 70% chocolate Valrhona • 30 g cocoa powder Valrhona •
30 g butter • 1 egg white • 25 g sugar • 1
sheet gelatin • 50 g heavy cream • 1 vanilla bean

In a bain marie heat the milk and the heavy
cream at 120 °F. Mix the sugar (keeping a
little bit to stabilize with the milk) and the
egg yolks together. Add the extra sugar to
the milk mixture in the bain marie to stabilize and then slowly add the remaining
sugar and yolk mixture to the bain marie.
Next, add the butter and the vanilla bean
and mix well. In a separate bowl, beat egg
whites and slowly fold into the bain marie
mixture. Add the cocoa powder. Bloom the
gelatin sheet in warm water. Once the gelatin is bloomed and all the excess water is
squeezed out, thoroughly stir the gelatin
into the warm bain marie mixture.

Teig
90 g Haselnüsse • 90 g Puderzucker • 10 g
Mehl • 120 g Eiweiß • 35 g Zucker

Haselnüsse für etwa 8 Minuten bei 160 °C
im Ofen rösten. Die abgekühlten Nüsse fein
mahlen. Puderzucker und Mehl zu den
gemahlenen Nüssen geben. Eiweiß und
Zucker zu Baiser schlagen. Nussmischung
von Hand vorsichtig unter die Baisermi-
schung rühren. In kleinen runden Förmchen
bei 160 °C für ca. 15–20 Minuten backen.

Praliné Feuilletine
60 g Valrhona Praliné • 30 g Feuilletine •
15 g Valrhona Jivara Milchschokolade

Schokolade im Wasserbad schmelzen und
Praliné dazugeben. Dann die Feuilletine
dazugeben und gut umrühren. Mischung auf
mit Backpapier ausgelegtem Backblech in
einer dünnen Schicht verteilen.

Schokoladenmousse
50 g Milch • 2 Eigelb • 60 g Valrhona
Schokolade 70% • 30 g Valrhona Kakaopulver • 30 g Butter • 1 Eiweiß • 25 g
Zucker • 1 Blatt Gelatine • 50 g Crème
fraîche • 1 Vanilleschote

Milch und Crème fraîche im Wasserbad bei
50 °C erhitzen. Zucker (etwas zur Stabilisie-
rung der Milch aufheben) und Eigelb vermischen. Restlichen Zucker zur Milchmischung
im Wasserbad geben, um sie zu stabilisie-
ren und danach langsam Zucker und Eigelb
dazugeben. Butter und Vanilleschote dazugeben und gut umrühren. In einer separaten
Schüssel das Eiweiß schlagen und nach
nach zu der Mischung im Wasserbad geben.
Kakaopulver dazugeben. Gelatineblatt in
warmem Wasser auflösen. Die aufgelöste
Gelatine ausdrücken und langsam in die
Mischung im Wasserbad einrühren.

Biscuit
90 g de noisettes • 90 g de sucre glace •
10 g de farine • 120 g de blancs d'œufs •
35 g de sucre

Grillez les noisettes au four à 160 °C pendant environ 8 minutes. Une fois refroidies,
les moudre en poudre fine. Ajoutez aux noisettes moulues le sucre en poudre et la
farine. Battre les blancs et le sucre pour
faire la meringue. Mélangez doucement et à
la main la meringue et la préparation à
base de noisettes. Mettez dans des petits
moules circulaires au four à 180 °C pendant
environ 15–20 minutes.

Praliné Feuilletine
00 g de pralin Valrhona • 30 g feuilletine •
15 g de chocolat au lait Valrhona Jivara

Faites fondre le chocolat au bain-marie.
Ajoutez d'abord le pralin puis la feuilletine
et mélangez bien. Versez le mélange sur
une plaque de cuisson recouverte de papier
sulfurisé et étalez en fine couche.

Mousse au chocolat
50 g de lait • 2 jaune d'œufs • 60 g de
chocolat Valrhona à 70% • 30 g de cacao
en poudre Valrhona • 30 g de beurre • 1
blanc d'œuf• 25 g de sucre • 1 feuille de
gélatine • 50 g de crème fraîche épaisse •
1 gousse de vanille

Chauffez au bain-marie le lait et la crème
fraîche épaisse à 80 °C. Mélangez le sucre
(gardez-en un peu pour stabiliser le lait) et
les jaunes ensemble. Ajoutez le sucre
restant au mélange lait et crème au bain-
marie pour stabiliser et ajoutez-y peu à peu
la préparation sucre et jaunes d'œufs.
Ajoutez ensuite le beurre et la gousse de
vanille et mélangez bien. Dans un autre bol,
battez les blancs et ajoutez-les doucement
à la préparation au bain-marie. Ajoutez le
cacao en poudre. Faites gonfler la feuille de
gélatine dans de l'eau chaude. Pressez la
gélatine pour en retirer l'excédent d'eau et
mélangez-la bien dans la préparation chaude au bain-marie.

Bizcocho
90 g de avellanas • 90 g de azúcar de
repostería • 10 g de harina • 12 huevos
blancos • 35 g de azúcar

Tostar las avellanas en el horno durante
unos 8 minutos a 160 °C. Una vez frías
molerlas hasta conseguir un polvo fino.
Añadir el azúcar de repostería y la harina.
Batir las claras de los huevos y el azúcar
para hacer merengue. Combinar el merengue con la mezcla de las avellanas y remover suavemente. Cocer en moldes individuales a 160 °C durante 15–20 minutos.

Feuilletine de praliné
60 g praliné Valrhona • 30 g de feuilletine •
15 g de chocolate con leche Valrhona Jivara

Derretir el chocolate al baño María. Añadir
el praliné y luego el feuilletine y remover.
Verter la mezcla en un recipiente plano y
repartir para conseguir una capa muy fina.

Mousse de chocolate
50 g de leche • 2 yemas de huevo • 60 g
de chocolate Valrhona 70% de cacao • 30 g
polvo de cacao Valrhona • 30 g de mantequilla • 1 clara de huevo • 25 g de azúcar •
1 hoja de gelatina • 50 g de nata espesa •
1 vaina de vainilla

Calentar la leche con la nata al baño María
a unos 80 °C. Mezclar el azúcar (guardar un
poquito para estabilizar la leche) con las
yemas. Añadir el azúcar extra a la mezcla
de leche y nata en el baño María para esta-
bilizarla. Entonces, añadir el azucar restante y la mezcla de yema al baño María.
Después, mezclar bien con la mantequilla y
la vaina de vainilla. En un recipiente aparte,
batir la clara a punto de nieve y añadir lentamente a la mezcla junto con el polvo de
cacao. Poner la hoja de gelatina en agua
caliente, y una vez reblandecida escurrir y
agregar al preparado.

Omen

Owner: Mikio Shinagawa

113 Thompson Street | New York, NY 10012
Phone: +1 212 925 8923
Subway: C and E to Spring Street
Opening hours: Daily 6 pm to 1 am
Average price: $16 – $48
Cuisine: Traditional Kyoto Style Cuisine

Udon Noodle Soup

Udon-Nudelsuppe
Soupe traditionnelle de nouilles
Sopa de fideos tradicional

- Seaweeds
- Sesame Seeds
- Scallions
- Ginger, shredded
- Eggplant, sliced
- Spinach, blanched
- White Raddish, shredded
- Burdock

In Japanese broth

- Algen
- Sesamsamen
- Frühlingszwiebeln
- Ingwer, klein gehackt
- Aubergine, in Scheiben geschnitten
- Spinat, blanchiert
- Weißer Rettich, gerieben
- Burdock (Große Klette)

In japanischer Brühe

- Algues de mer
- Graines de sésame
- Echalotes
- Gingembre émincé
- Aubergine en tranche
- Epinards blanchis
- Radis blanc émincé
- Bardane

Dans un bouillon japonais

- Algas
- Semillas de sésamo
- Cebolletas
- Jengibre en tiras
- Berenjena en rodajas
- Espinacas escaldadas
- Rábano en tiras
- Bardana

En caldo japonés

Pravda

Architect: Keith McNally and Ana Opitz | Chef: Peter Cheng

281 Lafayette Street | New York, NY 10012
Phone: +1 212 226 4944
www.pravdany.com, info@pravdany.com
Subway: 6 to Spring Street, N, R to Prince Street, B, F to Broadway/Lafayette Street
Opening hours: Sun–Tue 5 pm to 1 am, Wed–Thu 5 pm to 2 am, Fri–Sat 5 pm to 3 am
Cuisine: Underground caviar bar, cocktail & Martini bar with Russian
inspired food

Pravda's "Vodka Rack"

Pravdas „Wodka-Regal"
Le « panier de vodka » du Pravda
Vodka Rack del Pravda

A selection of six shots of vodka, always including one of our house-infused flavors.

The shots are served in a rectangle-shaped metal box which has the numbers 1–6 embossed on the side of the box, filled with crushed ice.
We send the rack with a small card, naming each shot and its country of origin.

Sechs ausgewählte Wodka-Shots, darunter immer eine unserer speziellen Haussorten.

Die Gläser werden in einer mit zerstoßenem Eis gefüllten rechteckigen Metallbox serviert, auf deren Seite die Zahlen 1–6 eingraviert sind.
Das Wodka-Regal wird zusammen mit einer kleinen Karte serviert, auf der die Wodkamarken und ihre Herkunftsländer aufgeführt sind.

C'est une sélection de six petits échantillons de vodka, comprenant toujours une de nos vodkas faite maison aux saveurs spéciales.

Les petits échantillons sont présentés dans une boîte en métal rectangulaire avec les numéros 1–6 gravés sur le côté de la boîte, remplie de glace pilée.
Nous envoyons le panier avec une étiquette sur chaque échantillon indiquant son nom et son pays d'origine.

Una selección de seis chupitos de vodka, que incluye siempre uno de los sabores de la casa.

Los chupitos se sirven en una caja de metal de forma triangular que tiene los números del uno al seis grabados en los laterales y está llena de hielo picado.
El combinado se presenta con una pequeña carta en la que se especifica el tipo de vodka y su lugar de origen.

Schiller's Liquor Bar

Architect: Keith McNally | Chef: Read Nasar, Lee Hanson

131 Rivington Street | New York, NY 10002
Phone: +1 212 260 4555
www.schillerny.com
Subway: F, J, M, Z to Delancey Street
Opening hours: Breakfast Mon–Fri 8 am to noon, Lunch Mon–Fri noon to 5 pm,
Brunch Sat–Sun 10 am to 5 pm, Dinner Daily 6 pm to 2 am
Average price: Breakfast items $2 – $9, Appetizers $6 – $8, Entrées $8 – $16
Cuisine: Continental with European influences

Schiller's

Casablanca Martini

Schiller's Casablanca Martini
Martini Casablanca de Schiller
Martini Casablanca de Schiller

60 ml Vodka Vanilla • 45 ml Pineapple juice • 30 ml Coconut paste • 2 dashes of Grenadine • 2 dashes of fresh lime juice

Shaken over ice, served with a strawberry.

60 ml Vanille-Wodka • 45 ml Ananassaft • 30 ml Kokosnussmark • 2 Spritzer Grenadine • 2 Spritzer frischen Limettensaft

Geschüttelt über Eis servieren, mit Erdbeere garnieren.

60 ml de Vodka vanille • 45 ml de jus d'ananas • 30 ml de crème de noix de coco • 2 gouttes de Grenadine • 2 gouttes de jus de citron vert frais

Mélangez et versez sur glace pilée. Servez avec une fraise.

60 ml de vodka vainilla • 45 ml de zumo de piña • 30 ml de pasta de coco • 2 chorritos de granadina • 2 chorritos de zumo de lima natural

Agitar, verter sobre hielo y servir con una fresa.

Strip House

Architect: Rockwell Group | Chef: David Walzog

13 East 12th Street (Greenwich Village) | New York, NY 10003
Phone: +1 212 328 0000
www.theglaziergroup.com
Subway: L, N, R, 4, 5, 6 to Union Square
Opening hours: Dinner Sun 5 pm to 10 pm, Mon–Thu 5 pm to 11 pm, Fri–Sat 5 pm
to 11:30 pm | Bar Sun until midnight, Mon–Thu until 2 am, Fri–Sat until 3 am
Average price: $22 – $37
Cuisine: Steakhouse with French flair

New York Strip Steak

Red freshly cut looking meat. For a good size steak it should be about 13/4"—2" thick steaks that weigh about 14–16 oz. The top layer of fat on the steak should be no more than 1/8" thick. Good "marbeling" of the steak, this is the fat that is naturally grained throughout the steak, as the steak cooks this fat renders and naturally tenderizes the steak and also builds in flavor.

To season and grill the steaks:
Season the steaks simply with ground black pepper and kosher salt.

To cook:
After knocking down the charcoal create a hot spot in the center of the grill. Place the seasoned steaks onto the grill right at the hot spot. To grill the steaks to have a charred exterior leave the steaks on an uncovered grill for the first 4–5 minutes. After this time, cover the grill, but don't go away, the grill will get very hot and the steaks may burn. Monitor the steaks every minute or two when the grill cover is closed. Once you have gotten close to the amount of char, check with an instant read thermometer the internal temperature of the steak. Medium rare—medium should be about 110 °F–120 °F. When the steaks are being cooked the meat contracts and becomes tight and the blood runs to the center of the steak. The steaks need time to rest before serving. This is about 4–5 minutes to allow the blood to come back to the edges of the meat and for the tissue of the meat to expand.

Blutiges, frisch geschnittenes Stück Fleisch. Ein gutes Steakstück sollte etwa 3 cm dick sein und um die 400 g wiegen. Die obere Fettschicht sollte nicht dicker als 0,8 cm sein. Die richtige Marmorierung des Steaks ist besonders wichtig. Darunter versteht man die Fettstränge, die durch das Fleischstück verlaufen. Beim Braten zerläuft dieses Fett und sorgt dafür, dass das Steak besonders zart und geschmackvoll ist.

Würzen und Grillen der Steaks:
Steaks einfach mit gemahlenem Pfeffer und koscherem Salz würzen.

Grillen:
Wenn die Grillkohle zusammengefallen ist, in der Mitte des Grills einen heißen Punkt schaffen und die gewürzten Steaks genau auf diese Stelle legen. Damit die Steaks eine gebräunte Außenhaut bekommen, den Grill die ersten 4–5 Minuten nicht abdecken. Danach den Grill abdecken, aber dabei stehen bleiben, denn der Grill wird sehr heiß und das Fleisch könnte anbrennen. Steaks unter abgedecktem Grill alle ein bis zwei Minuten kontrollieren. Wenn die Kohle fast runtergebrannt ist, mit einem Instant-Thermometer die Innentemperatur der Steaks messen. Halb rohe – medium Steaks sollten eine Temperatur von 40 °C– 50 °C haben. Beim Braten der Steaks zieht sich das Fleisch zusammen und wird straffer. Das Blut läuft dadurch zur Mitte des Steaks. Vor dem Servieren müssen die Steaks etwas ruhen gelassen werden. Es braucht etwa 4–5 Minuten, bis das Blut wieder in die Enden des Fleischstücks zurück geflossen ist und sich das Fleisch wieder ausgeweitet hat.

Viande fraîche bien rouge. Un steak de bonne taille doit avoir 3 cm d'épaisseur et peser 350–400 g. Le gras du steak ne doit pas faire plus de 0,8 cm d'épaisseur. Le steak doit être « bien marbré » de gras qui en cuisant attendri la viande et lui donne du goût.

Pour assaisonner et griller les steaks : Assaisonnez les steaks simplement avec du poivre noir moulu et du sel kosher.

La cuisson :
Ramenez un tas de braises au centre du gril pour créer une source de chaleur intense. Mettez les steaks assaisonnés sur le gril juste au-dessus de ce foyer. Pour avoir les steaks bien grillés laissez-les non couverts pendant les 4–5 premières minutes. Après cela, couvrez le gril et restez à côté, car il va devenir très chaud et les steaks pourraient brûler. Contrôlez les steaks toutes les 2 minutes quand le couvercle du gril est fermé. Contrôlez alors la température de l'intérieur du steak avec un thermomètre. Pour une cuisson mi-saignant et à point, il faut une temperature d'environ 40 °C–50 °C. Une fois que les steaks sont cuits, ils durcissent et le sang va vers le centre. Laissez-les reposer pendant 4–5 minutes avant de les servir pour que le sang reparte sur les côtés de la viande et que la chair se détende.

La carne roja debe estar recién cortada y es recomendable que cada bistec tenga una medida de unos 3 cm y pese unos 400 g. La capa de grasa que los recubre no debe superar el centímetro de espesor, y debería ser homogénea en toda la superficie de la pieza para que la cantidad que se desprenda durante la cocción le proporcione suficiente aroma y sabor.

Para aderezar y cocinar los bistecs:
Condimentar exclusivamente con pimienta negra y sal kosher.

La cocción:
Llevar las brasas al centro del fuego para crear una fuente de calor intensa. Colocar los bistecs sazonados justo encima de este punto. Para que presenten un aspecto exterior apetecible, dejarlos durante unos cuatro minutos. Inmediatamente, tapar la carne unos minutos más y controlar que la carne no se queme cada dos minutos. Verificar la temperatura del interior del bistec con un termómetro. Para una cocción media se necesita una temperatura entre unos 40 °C–50 °C. Cuando la carne está cocida expulsa sangre hacia el centro de la pieza. Antes de servirla, se recomienda dejarla reposar para que la sangre vuelva a impregnar cada uno los bistecs.

Suba

Architect: Andre Kikoski | Chef: Chris Santos

109 Ludlow Street (Lower East Side) | New York, NY 10002
Phone: +1 212 982 5714
www.subwaync.com
Subway: V to 2nd Avenue, F to Delancey Street
Opening hours: Dinner Sun–Wed 6 pm to 10:30 pm, Thu–Sat 6 pm to 23:30 pm |
Bar area Sun–Wed until 1 am, Thu until 2 am, Fri–Sat until 4 am
Average price: Appetizers $7 – $12, Entrées $17 – $25
Cuisine: Latin American, Spanish Tapas

Trout

with Polenta

Forelle mit Polenta
Truite à la polenta
Trucha con polenta

Boneless grilled trout served with grilled Serrano ham, soft tetilla cheese polenta and roasted chestnut, in lemongrass and basil emulsion.

Fish
Trout in filet: 8 oz, brush with oil and grill a la plancha.

Topping
2 oz sliced Serrano ham • 3 oz chestnuts • 0.5 oz sliced almonds • society garlic (small, blue flowers that taste like garlic)

Saute the chestnut in olive oil. Grill the Serrano ham. Roast almonds in the oven.

Polenta
0.4 oz Polenta • 3 oz vegetable stock • 2 oz skim milk • 1 oz tetilla cheese • ground cumin • ground coriander • ground celery salt • ground mace • salt

Heat the vegetable stock and the skim milk. Add the cumin, celery salt, mace, coriander, and salt. Add the polenta. Cook 8 minutes and then add the tetilla cheese.

Lemongrass and basil emulsion
0.5 oz shallots • 0.5 oz lemon grass • 0.5 oz ginger • 0.2 oz jalapeno • 0.2 oz olive oil • 0.2 oz basil • 4 oz vegetable stock • 1 oz skim milk

Heat the oil in a saucepan over medium-high heat. Add shallots and sauté until golden. Add the lemon grass, ginger, jalapeno and basil, and cook 2 minutes. Add the vegetable stock, skim milk and salt. Cook slowly for 25 minutes. Strain through a fine strainer and keep hot. Just before serving, beat with the emulsion blender.

Gegrillte Forelle ohne Gräten, mit Serrano-Schinken, Polenta mit mildem spanischem Tetilla-Käse und gerösteten Maronen, in Zitronengras-Basilikum-Emulsion.

Fisch
Filetierte Forelle: 250 g, mit Öl bestreichen und a la plancha grillen

Belag
60 g Serrano-Schinken in Streifen • 80 g Maronen • 20 g gehackte Mandeln • „Society"-Knoblauch (kleine, blaue Blüten, die wie Knoblauch schmecken)

Maronen in Olivenöl anbraten. Serrano-Schinken grillen. Mandeln im Ofen rösten.

Polenta
10 g Polenta • 80 ml Gemüsebrühe • 50 ml Magermilch • 30 g Tetilla-Käse • gemahlener Kreuzkümmel • gemahlener Koriander • gemahlenes Selleriesalz • gemahlene Muskatnuss • Salz

Gemüsebrühe und Milch erhitzen. Kreuzkümmel, Selleriesalz, Muskatblüte, Koriander und Salz dazugeben. Polenta dazugeben. 8 Minuten kochen lassen und dann den Tetilla-Käse hinzufügen.

Zitronengras-Basilikum-Emulsion
20 g Schalotten • 20 g Zitronengras • 20 g Ingwer • 5 g Jalapeno • 5 g Olivenöl • 5 g Basilikum • 120 ml Gemüsebrühe • 30 ml Magermilch

Öl auf mittlerer Stärke erhitzen. Schalotten goldgelb anbraten. Zitronengras, Ingwer, Jalapeno und Basilikum dazugeben und 2 Minuten kochen. Brühe, Milch und Salz dazugeben. Langsam 25 Minuten kochen lassen. Durch feines Sieb passieren und warm halten. Kurz vor dem Servieren mit Mixer aufschlagen.

Truite grillée sans arêtes servie avec du jambon Serrano, du fromage mou tetilla, de la polenta et des marrons grillés dans une émulsion de citronnelle et basilic.

Poisson
filet de truite : 250 g frotté avec de l'huile et grillé à la plancha.

Garniture
60 g de Serrano en tranche • 80 g de marrons • 20 g d'amandes émincées • ail « society » (petites fleurs bleues au goût d'ail)

Faites revenir marrons dans l'huile d'olive. Grillez le jambon Serrano. Grillez amandes.

Polenta
10 g de Polenta • 80 ml de bouillon de légumes • 50 ml de lait écrémé • 30 g de fromage tetilla • cumin moulu • coriandre moulue • sel de céleri • macis moulu • sel

Chauffez le bouillon de légumes et le lait écrémé. Ajoutez le cumin, le sel de céleri, le macis, la coriandre et le sel. Ajoutez la polenta. Cuisinez 8 minutes et ajoutez ensuite le tetilla.

Emulsion de citronnelle et basilic
20 g d'échalotes • 20 g de citronnelle • 20 g de gingembre • 5 g de Jalapeño • 5 g d'huile d'olive • 5 g basilic • 120 ml de bouillon de légume • 30 ml de lait écrémé

Chauffez l'huile dans une casserole à feu vif moyen. Ajoutez les échalotes et faites dorer. Ajoutez la citronnelle, le gingembre, le jalapeno et le basilic et faites cuire pendant 2 minutes. Ajoutez le bouillon de légumes, le lait écrémé et le sel. Faites cuire doucement pendant 25 minutes. Passez au chinois et gardez chaud. Donnez un coup de fouet, avant de servir.

Trucha sin espina a la plancha servida con jamón serrano, polenta de queso de tetilla y castañas tostadas, con una emulsión de lemongrass y albahaca.

Pescado
Filetes de trucha: 250 g de filetes pintados con aceite y asados a la plancha

Guarnición
60 g de jamón serrano • 80 g de castañas • 20 g de almendras en láminas • flores de ajo (pequeñas flores azules que saben a ajo)

Saltear las castañas en aceite de oliva. Tostar el jamón serrano y almendras en el horno.

Polenta
10 g de polenta • 80 ml de caldo vegetal • 50 ml de leche desnatada • 30 g de queso de tetilla • comino • cilantro • sal de apio • nuez moscada • sal

Calentar el caldo vegetal y la leche desnatada. Añadir el comino, la sal de apio, la nuez moscada, el cilantro, la sal y la polenta. Cocer durante 8 minutos y luego añadir el queso de tetilla.

Emulsión de lemongrass y albahaca
20 g de cebolletas • 20 g de lemongrass • 20 g de jengibre • 5 g de jalapeño • 5 g de aceite de oliva • 5 g de albahaca • 120 ml de caldo vegetal • 30 ml de leche desnatada

Calentar el aceite en una sartén a fuego medio. Saltear las cebolletas hasta que estén doradas. Añadir el lemongrass, el jengibre, el jalapeño, el cilantro y cocer durante 2 minutos. Añadir el caldo, la leche desnatada y la sal. Cocer a fuego lento 25 minutos más. Colar en un colador fino mantener caliente. Justo antes de ser batir la emulsión.

Su

Thom's Bar

Architect: Stephen B Jacobs Group PC, Thomas O'Brien,
Aero Studios | Chef: Jonathan Eismann

Hotel 60 Thompson | 60 Thompson Street | New York, NY 10012
Phone: +1 877 431 04 00
www.60thompson.com
Subway: E, C to Spring Street
Opening hours: 6:30 am to 23:30 pm
Average price: $18 – $28
Cuisine: American with Asian touch

Thom's Bar

Chai
Martini

3 oz sky vanilla
2 oz chai tea (oregon chai, vanilla & honey)
Splash of milk

Shaken, served up in a martini glass.
Cinnamon stick as a garnish.

80 g Sky Vanilla
50 g Chai-Tee (Oregon Chai, Vanille und Honig)
Ein Spritzer Milch

Geschüttelt, serviert im Martini-Glas.
Zimtstange als Garnierung.

80 g de vanille « sky »
50 g de thé chai (chai orégon, vanille & miel)
Quelques gouttes de lait

Mélangez dans le shaker, servez dans un verre à Martini.
Garnissez de bâton de cannelle.

80 g de vainilla
50 g de té chai (oregón chai, vainilla y miel)
Un chorro de leche

Agitar todos los ingredientes y servir en vaso de martini.
Emplear un palito de canela como adorno.

Town

Architect: David Rockwell | Chef: Luci Levere

15 West 56th Street | New York, NY 10019
Phone: +1 212 582 4445
www.townnyc.com
Subway: E, V to 5th Avenue/53rd Street, N, R, W to 5th Avenue/59th Street
Opening hours: Mon–Thu 7 am to 10:30 am, noon to 2 pm, 5:30 pm to 10:30 pm,
Fri until 11 pm, Sat 7 am to 10:30 am, 5:30 pm to 11 pm, Sun 11 am to 2 pm,
5:30 pm to 10:30 pm
Cuisine: American dynamic, inspired by season and market

Appetizers

Appetithappen
Amuse-gueules
Aperitivos

Entrees are one spirited and refined with selections such as Duck steak • Fragrant endive • Soba buckwheat • Rib eye with ribs • Swiss chard gratin • Pommes puree • Marrow soufflé

Signature dishes:

Fall
Diver scallop • Scallop sausage • Ginger lettuce

Winter
Roasted venison loin • Celery and truffles • Quinces • Wild striped bass • Organic red lentils • Horseradish shiraz sauce

Spring
Jumbo white asparagus in their own juice with fenel • Blood orange reduction • Soft shell crab • Braised endive • Golden raisins • Crab coulis

Summer
Fete watermelon • Heirloom tomato salad • Soft shell crab • Braised endive • Golden raisins • Crab coulis

Anytime
Risotto of escargots • Sweet garlic • Black truffle essence • Octopus (lightly grilled) • Potato and lemon grass broth

Bei der Vorspeise hat man die Wahl zwischen ausgesuchten Gerichten wie beispielsweise Entensteak • Würzige Endivien • Soba-Buchweizennudeln • Rib-Eye-Steak mit Knochen • Mangoldgratin nach Schweizer Art • Kartoffelpüree • Kürbissoufflé

Saison-Gerichte:

Herbst
Jakobsmuschel • Jakobsmuschelwurst • Ingwer-Salat

Winter
Rehrückenbraten • Sellerie und Trüffel • Quitten • Wilder Felsenbarsch • Rote Bio-Linsen • Shiraz-Meerrettichsoße

Frühling
Weißer Jumbospargel im eigenen Saft mit Fenchel • Blutorangen-Reduktion • Weich-schalenkrebs • Geschmorte Endivie • Goldrosinen • Krebscreme

Sommer
Wassermelone • Salat aus Heirloom-Tomaten • Weichschalenkrebs • Geschmorte Endivie • Goldrosinen • Krebscreme

Das ganze Jahr über
Risotto mit Schnecken • Süßer Knoblauch • Essenz aus schwarzen Trüffeln • Tintenfisch (leicht gegrillt) • Brühe aus Kartoffeln und Zitronengras

Entrées composées de délicatesses à thème unique, fines et raffinées Steak de canard • Endives parfumées • Galette de blé noir de soba • Entrecôte avec la côte • Gratin de bettes • Purée de pommes de terre • Soufflé de courge

Plat à thème :

Automne
Noix de St Jacques du plongeur • Quenelle de noix de St Jacques • Laitue au gingembre

Hiver
Filet de venaison grillé • Céleri et truffes • Coings • Bar rayé sauvage • Lentilles rouges biologiques • Sauce de raifort shiraz

Printemps
Asperges blanches géantes en sauce et fenouil • Réduction d'orange sanguine • Crabe mou• Endives braisées • Raisins dorés • Coulis de crabe

Eté
Pastèque de fête • Salade de tomate du patrimoine • Crabe mou • Endives braisées • Raisins dorés • Coulis de crabe

Toutes saisons
Risotto d'escargots • Ail doux • Essence de truffe noir • Poulpe (légèrement grillé) • bouillon de pommes de terre et citronnelle

Los entrantes contienen refinados ingredientes como Bistec de pato • Endivia fragante • Fideos de trigo sarraceno • Bistec de punta de lomo • Remolacha gratinada • Puré de patata • Soufflé de calabaza

Platos según temporada:

Otoño
Vieira pescada de forma artesanal • Salchicha de vieira • Lechuga con jengibre

Invierno
Asado de carne de venado • Apio y trufas • Membrillo • Róbalo rayado • Lentillas rojas ecológicas • Salsa de rábanos

Primavera
Espárragos gigantes blancos en su propio jugo con hinojo • Emulsión de naranja sanguina • Cangrejo • Endibias estofadas • Uvas pasas • Pudin de cangrejo

Verano
Sandía • Ensalada de tomate •Cangrejo • Endibias asadas • Uvas pasas • Pudin de cangrejo

En cualquier época
Arroz con caracoles • Ajo dulce • Esencia de trufas negras • Pulpo asado • Sopa de patatas y hierba de limón

66

Architect: Richard Meier | Executive Chefs: Jean-Georges
Vongerichten, Phil Suarez

241 Church Street | New York, NY 10013
Phone +1 212 925 0202
Subway: Canal Street
Average price: $18 – $38
Cuisine: Chinese with a twist

Hudson River

SOHO

Canal Street

5

26

FINANCIAL
DISTRICT

17

Broadway

20 Lafayette Stree

19 24

1

Houston Street

21

23

LOWER EAST SID

Brooklyn Bridge

Manhattan Bridge

BROOKLYN

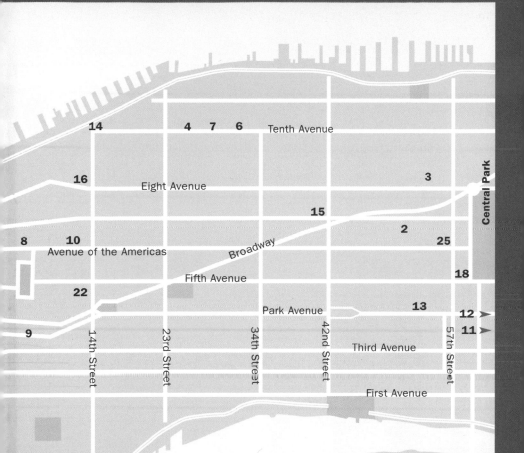

14　　　　4　7　6　Tenth Avenue

16　　　Eight Avenue　　　　　　　　　　3　Central Park

15

8　　10　　　　　　　　　　　　2
Avenue of the Americas　　Broadway　　　25

Fifth Avenue　　　　　　　　　　　18

22　　　　　　Park Avenue　　13　　12 ➤

9　　　　　　　　　　　　　　　11 ➤

14th Street　23rd Street　34th Street　42nd Street　Third Avenue　57th Street

First Avenue

East River

QUEENS

Published in the same series:

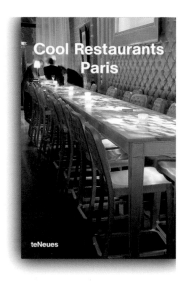

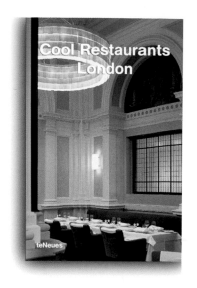

Size: 14 x 21.5 cm / 5½ x 8 in.
136 pp
Flexicover
c. 100 color photographs
Text in English, German, French
and Spanish
ISBN 3-8238-4570-5

Size: 14 x 21.5 cm / 5½ x 8 in.
136 pp
Flexicover
c. 100 color photographs
Text in English, German, French
and Spanish
ISBN 3-8238-4568-3

To be published in the same series:

Amsterdam
Barcelona
Berlin
Brussels
Chicago
Los Angeles

Madrid
Miami
Milan
Moscow
Tokyo